Masters of the Matrix

Becoming the Architect of Your Reality and
Activating the Original Human Template

Magenta Pixie

About the Author

Magenta Pixie is a channel for the higher dimensional, divine intelligence known as 'The White Winged Collective Consciousness of Nine'. The transmissions she receives from 'The Nine' have reached thousands of people worldwide via the extensive video collection on her YouTube channel. She has worked with people from all over the world as an intuitive consultant and holistic life coach. Magenta lives in the New Forest, UK with her partner, her son, one dog and two cats.

Visit Magenta Pixie online at www.magentapixie.com

Cover design by Daniel Saunders
Author photograph by Oliver McGuire

Print Edition 1.1, 2016

ISBN-13: 978-1539080015
ISBN-10: 1539080013

White Spirit Publishing
www.magentapixie.com
enquiries: catzmagick@mail.com

This book is dedicated to my children and grandchildren.
You are the light in my life, and the love in my heart.
You complete the circle, and stand with me throughout infinity.
My love for you knows no bounds.
Alex, Abby, Rosie, Ollie, Christian, Gracie, Imogen, Riley, Rody, Elora... and
all the other souls yet to incarnate into our family tree.

And to you, dear reader, I dedicate this book to *your* children,
grandchildren, nieces and nephews. For they are our future. They are the
lightbringers, and dreamweavers of the web. They carry the crystalline
codes for the new dawn. They are the Masters of the Matrix.

Contents

Acknowledgements

Special thanks to Dee Taylor-Mason and Heike Jenkins for listening to my endless chatter about the 'geometric transmissions' that became this work. Your belief and enthusiasm has been invaluable in the writing of this material, and I am so grateful for your continued friendship.

To my father, Brian McGuire, my greatest mentor. You are the best Daddy a girl could wish for.

To Gordon Blake, who knew I would write a book long before I did. I have never forgotten your vision.

Also to my editor and love of my life, Daniel. Without your never-ending support and encouragement, this book might not have made it into the public domain. You are appreciated more than you know!

Introduction

The time has come in our current reality to awaken to the truth of our existence and to discover who we truly are.

That discovery can only take place from a journey inward, to the place we call 'within' or 'inner space'.

It is a journey through the vast expanse of our imagination. In this lies the key to our past, present and future and the answers to every question we have ever asked ourselves.

There is no book, film, person or teacher that can unravel these mysteries for us. We are each our own gurus, guides and masters. We are each our own libraries and computer systems. The books, films, people and teachers are simply keys. They are there to help us unlock the doors to this vast dimension that we call our imagination.

This is one such book. A key. A 'trigger' or a 'code', if you will. Yet you are the one that shall do the work of unravelling the mysteries within; decoding your own metaphors, translating symbols into your own language, rewriting your past, present and future, if you so wish, and creating your destiny.

"The best place to start is always at the beginning," they say; but when it comes to the true fabric of reality, there are no beginnings, middles or endings. Time and space is one never-ending circle or, more accurately, 'spiral'. So let us begin somewhere upon that spiral and jump straight in.

I communicate with what I now know is a deeper aspect of myself. An aspect of 'the all'.

Indeed 'the all' is what I am communicating with. It only presents as an aspect as it comes through me, and my own perception of myself is that of an aspect within the all. A tiny piece of the overall macrocosm of life.

'They' say I am 'all and everything'. I am that macrocosm and, of course, so are you!

This 'aspect of myself' originally came to me as one spirit being. A being that I could see and feel and hear within that 'inner space' inside my mind.

It was like my mind was a little room, and that room was just one small part of this vast space that I called my mind, that I did not understand.

In this room, which I had been aware of since I was around thirteen years old, this spirit being would visit me and talk to me. He would answer pretty much every question I had.

He told me his name was "White Spirit", and he presented his form to me as a Zulu warrior. He said he was a 'past life version of myself' and was from the 'fifth dimension'.

I first made contact with White Spirit in meditation but after a while I began to see, feel and hear him in my everyday life. It was strange at first; communicating with this other-worldly, non-physical being. But I loved the communication.

The amount of love and joy that would flow through my entire being when I was communicating with White Spirit was astounding. I had never felt anything like it before. The nearest thing I had ever experienced to this was being on stage performing. I had been involved in drama and acting since I was a child. Anyone who is creative will know the 'high' this brings, but communicating with White Spirit was even more profound and euphoric.

My questions for White Spirit became more and more complex. I wanted to know everything. Who was he? What did he mean when he said he was a past life version of me? Where was the fifth dimension? Why was he communicating with me?

All these and many more questions were answered, leading of course, to yet more questions.

One day, after I had asked White Spirit a particularly abstract question, he simply replied, "I don't know."

He then told me that he could go and find out the answer if I wanted.

I agreed to this, and I was really intrigued as to why he did not know. I thought he knew everything!

I watched White Spirit disappear up a rainbow coloured ladder, through a portal in the roof of the little room in my mind. He was gone for a good few minutes or so. When he came back, he had the answer to my question but that hardly mattered to me any more. All I wanted to know was, where did he go? Who was it that he asked to get the answer, and why didn't he know the answer himself?

White Spirit explained that whilst he was a guide for me, he too had a guide of his own in a higher dimension. He needed to 'go higher' in order to retrieve the answer to that particular question.

I worked with White Spirit for around seven years. In that time he taught me so much, and he attempted to answer all of my questions. If he did not know the answer then he would climb up that rainbow coloured ladder and come back a few minutes later with the answer.

Sometimes I cut off my communication with White Spirit. When I was going through challenging situations in my life I would simply 'forget' to talk to him, or I would try to talk to him but I could not see him, or that little room, in my mind.

Other times, he would come back and we would have intensive communication sessions for days at a time. Often when this happened, I would shut myself away at home so I could focus on constant and intense communications with White Spirit.

After around seven years of working with White Spirit, he told me I would be getting a 'new guide'.

He said that our time together, with him as the presentation of the Zulu warrior, had come to an end. I was upset about this as I had grown to love him and trust him, but he explained that both himself and the new guide were both aspects of me. He said that the new guide was a future version of myself, rather than a past version.

This 'upgrade moment' was a huge shift for me within that 'space in my mind'.

Since I was thirteen years old, I had held the awareness of this little room; and for the last seven years the room had been filled with White Spirit's presence.

Sometimes, many other beings (usually human relatives of people I had met) would knock on the door of the little room. They would want to come in and talk to their relative who was still living in the physical realm. This might be a lady sat over the other side of the coffee shop, or someone pushing a trolley around the same supermarket as me.

White Spirit acted as a 'gatekeeper' or a 'doorkeeper' within that room, and he would rarely let one of the other people in. He would explain to them that I was 'in training' and usually the people would leave.

White Spirit explained that they could 'see my light'; which meant that they knew I was able to communicate with them, and that I could act as a medium between these spirit people and physical living humans. On rare occasions, he would let one of the spirit people through. I would then speak to the human relative, acting as a medium or mediator between the spirit person in the little room and the physical person.

However, most of the time he did not let them through. He would say that I was 'in training' and the spirit people appeared to understand.

I asked White Spirit to explain to me what it was that I was in training for. He told me that I would be a 'medium for other mediums'.

He said that one day I would be speaking to lots of people all over the world, and that these people would mostly live in America. I was shown visions of myself wearing headphones and speaking into a microphone, and I knew there were lots of people listening. The computers back in the early 1990s were nothing like they are now, so I did not understand the nature of these visions at the time.

It was a profound moment for me when not only did White Spirit 'transform', but so did the little room in my mind that I had seen since I was thirteen years old!

That 'space' in my mind was replaced with a vast meadow, with trees, streams and rivers. There were coloured fish swimming in the rivers, and there were fluffy rabbits of all colours running about on the grass. Sometimes I saw gnomes, elves and pixies in the trees and I saw fairies flying around. There were other meadows beyond this one where I knew unicorns existed, but I could not see that far or access those meadows at that time.

The guide that White Spirit transformed into was a white winged being that I recognised as an angel. He acted as a 'gatekeeper' within this meadow, just as White Spirit had within the little room.

Sometimes this angel would present as 'just a man'.

He would lose the white wings and would be wearing blue denim jeans and a white t-shirt. He explained that he was still 'White Spirit', but he was an 'upgraded version'.

He also told me that, from a different perspective, he was an entirely separate entity from White Spirit.

After a few weeks of communicating with this angelic/human spirit entity, one day he just separated himself into several identical aspects. He explained that his true form was that of a 'collective'.

I began to refer to him as 'they' instead of 'him'.

I counted these aspects and there were nine of them.

Sometimes they would present as nine, white-winged, angelic beings. Sometimes their faces were not human; they looked similar to large birds. Other times, they had gentle human faces with long hair and they were all male.

Sometimes they were identical to one another, and other times they were all different.

There were times when they presented as nine young men wearing jeans and white t-shirts. On a few occasions, one of them would wear a black t-shirt or they would all wear different coloured t-shirts.

The only times I ever saw one of them transform into a female was if I was really upset about something in my life. On these occasions, a pure white goddess would come forward and all the males would take a step back to let her through. I was told that she was the 'divine feminine aspect', and she would come to bring me comfort and healing. She would talk to me very gently and I absolutely loved her. Most of the time though, they were all male.

I asked them why they changed form so often and they would answer that they were 'fluid', 'ever changing' and 'non-static'. They explained that their changing form was in alignment with my own understanding, awareness and expansion.

I did ask them which form was their true form. They told me that I could not see their true form, but that they could show me forms that were closest to their true presentation. I expressed that I wanted to see these closer forms and it was at this point that the landscape of 'the meadow' changed once again, and within that 'space in my mind' I saw what I can only describe as 'space'.

I saw galaxies, stars, universes, planets within a 'blackness' that also held bursts of colour. The forms of 'The Nine' changed into intricate geometric shapes, brightly coloured crystal structures, flashes of rainbow lights, electrical silver lines and rods. I saw a giant matrix, or web. I also saw hieroglyphs moving around, forming into what I knew was a language.

I also heard the sounds of this new landscape. I could hear musical notes, and what I can only describe as 'frequencies'.

The Nine explained that they were as much 'sounds' as they were a shape or a structure.

I loved watching these ever changing, fluid and most interesting forms. But at that time, I was more comfortable with their presentation as white, winged beings in the fairy meadow.

"Do you guys have names?" I asked them one day.

They said that the nearest they had to a name were the musical notes and frequencies that I had heard. They suggested *I* gave them a name, so I decided to call them... 'The White, Winged, Collective, Consciousness of Nine'.

This name or title seemed to best explain their presentation, and I knew for some reason that it was very important that they were white, winged and a collective consciousness. It was also very significant that they were presented as 'Nine'.

'The Nine' appeared quite comfortable with the label of 'The White, Winged, Collective, Consciousness of Nine'.

They did laugh when I chose the name though. In fact, they often laughed at things I said to them. They laughed at lots of my questions and often I did not get the joke, as I thought my questions were really serious!

They explained to me that the universal space and time they exist within was one of the 'funniest places' to be. They told me that humour was a predominant energy in the higher dimensions.

So, my communications into the spirit/imagination realms had 'upgraded'; and the presentation transmuted and transformed from 'White Spirit', the Zulu warrior in the little room, into 'The Nine' in the fairy meadow.

They referred to this 'space in my mind' as 'hyperspace'.

In the year 2008, I started to release the 'messages' from The Nine in video form on YouTube.

Since that time, I have conversed and communicated with these beings many times.

I know that 'The White, Winged, Collective, Consciousness of Nine' has to be the longest name for a spirit guide out there! Perhaps that is why they were laughing?

I now affectionately refer to them as 'The Nine'.

It appears that there are an infinite number of ways to express what is essentially one main message: that of our sovereignty as human beings.

The Nine are here to assist us in realising who we are, and to help and guide us into reclaiming that sovereign state. I am told that we, as humans, are wonderful beings. Each and every one of us.

We are all a unique representation of the 'one true source', 'divine creator' or 'God'; whichever phrase you wish to use. Many of us have forgotten who we are. Some of us know who we are, but we do not understand the significance of it.

Our planet is changing. Our planet is set upon a course of continued change. We are also changing. From the Nine's perspective, we are changing rapidly when it comes to growth and evolution within a physical existence.

Currently, we are within a 'growth spike'. This is where everything evolves in an exponential way compared to the usual evolutionary growth patterns. These 'spikes' occur regularly every 26,000 years, and our year of 2012 was the highest point of that evolutionary spike. Specifically, the winter solstice of December 21st 2012.

We are now on the 'other side' of that spike in a 'declining' phase, which is actually a phase of new creation. We are standing upon a blank page and we are writing a new history for ourselves. The Nine liken this to going 'beyond the rainbow', which they say is a metaphor 'in alignment with truth'.

These words are written here specifically to invoke higher thinking and creative processes. The expanded aspect of self, that I refer to as 'The Nine', works with evoking imagery within the reader in order for expansion and the creativity of one's own reality to take place.

The Nine communicate through specific codes within 'energy packets', which I perceive as 'downloads of information' that I then translate into the most appropriate words or terminology for the particular energy or vibration.

This, The Nine tell me, is the 'language of light'. If I look closer within the 'energy package', I can see a cloud-like smoke or mist with various colours and I can make out geometric symbols and shapes. I do not just 'see' these energy packages, I can hear them and feel them emotionally as well. When I translate the energy package, I use visuals, hearing and emotions which all come to me simultaneously.

Anyone who is reading these words does not need to understand them, or necessarily need to process them. Understanding and processing is important if you are one of those people who want to know why things work the way they do, but it is not needed for the receiving of the message or 'the codes' within these words.

The processing of the language of light is a 'left hemisphere of the brain' activity. This assists in sorting, evaluating, processing and understanding. However, it is not needed in order for the language of light to be communicated and for the recipient of the language of light codes to begin the activation or creativity. This is a 'right hemisphere of the brain' activity.

The Nine have a message. They came forward with a very large 'geometric energy package', much larger than the ones that I see when transcribing videos for YouTube.

I realised that this was going to be a longer piece of work, and that it would be presented as a book this time. They gave me the title before I even began to translate the download. The title they gave me was "Masters of the Matrix".

So I will now hand over the metaphoric quill to 'The Nine'.

I remain their receiver, transmitter and translator; and for you, the reader, I am eternally your scribe.

Magenta Pixie

1. The Past Life Contract and the Blueprint of Reality

What are 'past life contracts'? Why would we make one? How do we make one? Are we conscious of making them? Can they be made against our will, or without our knowledge? Can we break them? Are past life contracts negative or positive? How can we tell if we have any?

Firstly we would present to you what they are, and for this understanding, and indeed the processing of the concept, one would need to look with the multidimensional eye. Or indeed one would need to 'think' multidimensionally.

In a linear sense, contracts (or agreements) will have been made, either within the actual physical incarnation or from the vantage point of the non-physical-non-temporal self, or indeed both.

When one comes into an incarnation then these contracts or agreements are in place.

You ask how these contracts are created?

From the non-physical perspective, these are part of an 'energetic plan' if you will. The preincarnate blueprint. The 'map' of your lifetime. Within this map one will have laid out meetings, situations, individuals, emotions, all conducive to maximum growth and expansion for the individual at both the physical and the soul level. However, this is often not apparent from the physical perspective.

These contracts or agreements take place at an energetic level. This is energy connecting with energy, consciousness connecting with consciousness.

For those who think and see in geometric terms, one could visualise geometry fitting into place with geometry, like a jigsaw puzzle or Rubik's Cube.

The shape one would visualise would be hexagonal, yet there are other geometric shapes involved. To visualise the geometry connecting together brings you to the highest truth of this concept, with the least distortion.

For those who think and see within a fifth dimensional landscape (no less truthful, even if distortion is 'changed' shall we say?), one could visualise the 'Rainbow Bridge'.

The Rainbow Bridge

One walks across this Rainbow Bridge from one glorious meadow to the next. This would be an aligned metaphoric visual to this process, for this is about connection. The 'bridge' is that which connects one place to another.

For those who think and see in archetypal terms, one could visualise the higher being of light in the white robe and the lower being of darkness in the black robe. Both of equal import in deciding the map (or blueprint) of the individual.

Between them, the being of light and the being of darkness create a contract. They shake hands upon the agreement they have made.

All these; the geometric connections, the Rainbow Bridge, and the beings creating an agreement; all these are most aligned metaphors for the creating of the contract process.

Yet in truth, this is energetic and the geometry fitting together is the highest metaphor here.

Each visual will act as keys, codes and triggers to unlocking the cellular memories within your own DNA so that you may move into the fractal that is your 'past life contracts'.

As you move into this fractal, you find yourself within a web that surrounds you. A web that is available to you. The most aligned terminologies for this web would be 'matrix' or 'grid' from our perspective.

When scanning your language and the universal interpretations of them, 'matrix' or 'grid' are most high approximations. Yet there are other more scientific terminologies that would also fit most well, yet these are outside of the awareness of our conduit.

We may impart to the scientific and technological thinkers amongst you that these are number sequences related to your binary coding.

The number sequences would be of the highest alignment to explain and present that which we speak of. That which we speak of is the 'preincarnate blueprint', 'web' or 'map'.

When you look at the number sequences and the binary coding of the map, you will see that they do not sit within the field of the past at all but are presented always as the now through the position of the central point. The Zero Point field.

When one can conceptualise these sequences, one can process most well the past, present and future contracts outside of the linear line. For you ask us how you can break these contracts, and how you can create yet more contracts if you so choose to do so?

The answer to this lies within the central point of the field, the Zero Point, when looking at the number sequences we speak of.

Yet still we respond to your first question of, what are past life contracts?

If we refer to the preincarnate blueprint or map of your reality as a 'matrix' or 'grid', one can see that this matrix acts like a 'large computer' if you will.

Information may be inputted into this computer and information may be received from this computer.

This large computer, this matrix around you begins to devise coordinates, directions and maps for your lifetime and your reality. Your every thought, your every emotion is taken into this giant computer. Each thought, each emotion is a code so that this giant computer may present its technology to you. Technology that shall lead you into a certain direction in your life, in your reality, both as an incarnated physical being and as a soul.

This computer works away in the background. Sorting, filing, categorising and organising your life and all that you are. It produces the coordinates and maps to where you have been, where you are now and where you should go. Or could go.

Of course, this computer is you. Part of you. It is your 'bodymind'. Yet without awareness of it, it takes the lead in deciding which coordinates and maps would be best for you to follow.

You all have these large computers. Each and every one of you have these matrices of light and knowledge, information and power around you and within you.

Awareness

Yet with awareness, something changes. The computer no longer acts independently, deciding what it feels is for your highest good. The computer waits upon your signal, your input.

You program the computer yourself! You design the maps, you create the coordinates, and you decide where you shall go and what you shall do.

The computer, the 'matrix', works then at your bidding. Knowing that you know 'that which is your highest good'.

In a linear presentation, many of the contracts were made in the past. By the computer, by the matrix. Not against your will, but for the highest good.

Yet there is more to this story. There are those upon your planet who discovered (or were given) the technology to program the computers of others.

Whilst the physical incarnated individuals 'lay sleeping', those who had the technology began to program the computers. The sleeping physically incarnated individuals were unaware that those who had the technology, programmed the computers; the matrices to follow coordinates, plans and maps of their own choosing.

Those choices were not in the highest good of humanity. They were for the benefit of the programmers, so they may gain sustenance on all levels, to the the detriment of the physically incarnated individuals.

Masters of Your Matrix

This situation is not one that lies in your past, but in your present and potentially in your future. Only by 'awakening from the slumber' and 'becoming aware' can you program your own computer and become masters of your own matrix. The past life contracts are a crucial aspect of this. Understanding and processing what the 'past life contract' means is of the utmost import here.

For yes, indeed you created contracts and agreements for your highest good and for the good of all. So too did you create contracts that served you at the time, yet serve you no longer. So too were contracts created for you, by the computer itself, 'the matrix'. And by the others who learned to bypass protocols and access your computer and control it.

One must now decide which contract is which? Which ones to keep? Which ones to free oneself from? Which ones to newly create? Can one do this?

Yes indeed. To do this, one gains 'mastery over their matrix' and becomes a 'master of the matrix'.

How does one do this? There are many ways. All so accessible, all so available to you.

We shall come to this point.

So let us recap. The past life contract is 'energy meeting energy', geometries clicking into place, to create the 'map' or 'grid'. The large computer mind. The matrix.

Each and every one of you have this matrix. You are this computer. It is you.

You

The gridwork, patterns, codes, mathematical equations and number sequences click into place and thus, when this process is ready, 'you' are created.

Your inception point as a soul begins and you are born into physicality.

At the end of each incarnation you renew your matrix. Remove segments not needed, 'add new parts' if you will, program in new coordinates. You begin again, born anew into a new life with a new set of codes programmed into your matrix. The idea here is that your matrix grows, accumulating knowledge.

Moving further and further along the sequences of numbers, into the fractal. Exploring more and more of itself, expanding and upgrading; much like your technology of today.

One always wishes to move higher, to be faster, more efficient, to have more technology at one's fingertips. This is the journey of the soul, the matrix. Unlike your technology of today, the matrix always programs itself for your highest good on all levels.

Yet as we have told, the matrix can be hijacked, albeit temporarily. Yet if you have your 'anti-hijacking software' in place, this cannot happen and it will not happen.

How do you ensure anti-hijacking software is in place? By ensuring you obtain mastery over your matrix. By you becoming a 'master of the matrix'.

We, the White Winged Collective Consciousness of Nine, are here with you, through our conduit Magenta Pixie, to show you how.

2. The Twin Flame Contract

You ask the reasons for choosing to make a contract within your past life?

As we have said, the choice is not always made from the aspect of self that holds linear awareness.

Yet contracts are made from the linear perspective, often without the realisation that one is even making a contract!

For example... the marriage within the linear perception between one person and another is indeed a contract. It is a contract within the third dimension. This contract may or may not be mirrored upon other dimensions.

If the couple are soulmates or indeed 'twin souls'/'twin flames', then the contract will be made throughout the higher dimensions.

In the case of the couple who are not soulmates, the contract is made from the moment of the marriage. We speak here from the linear perspective.

In the case of soulmates or 'twin flames', when was the contract actually made? From a linear viewpoint it will almost certainly have been made within a 'past life'.

Yet from the multidimensional viewpoint, with both partners holding higher dimensional awareness, the contract is made from the 'now moment' (the Zero Point).

Is the 'now moment' the moment of the actual marriage, as in the case of the non-soulmate couple? The answer to this is yes and no. For the present (without higher dimensional awareness within either partner) still sits within linear time, for it is perceived as a 'moment between the past and the present'. There is still a linear flow to the moment if higher dimensional awareness is not experienced.

The Zero Point is a moment outside of linear time. The codons within the matrix will operate within a 'vertical line' rather than a 'horizontal one'. Therefore the matrix clicks the geometries 'upwards' if you will, through a multidimensional field (rather than the horizontal linear expression).

The 'contract', as in the marriage between the soulmate/twin flame aware couple, is 'locked into' many lifetimes until such time as the couple agree, on a conscious level, to break the contract.

True twin flame couples will be most unlikely to make such a choice, yet the complexity of the matrix is never simple to understand from the linear perspective. Only by experiencing the 'silence' and the 'simplicity' of the Zero Point can one hope to experience the complexity of the matrix, allowing processing and understanding of it to then occur.

The twin flame couple create bonds very difficult to break. Hence twin flames meeting in other lifetimes, already married to other partners, feeling as though they are still married to the twin flame.

In actuality this is truth. The marriage lasts far longer than one incarnation. We also have the happily married individual who feels as though he or she is missing someone they have never met. They are, in all intents and purposes 'in love' with the current spouse. This is the case with twin flame marriages in other lifetimes, or having created a 'contracted merge', who have not yet met in the current lifetime.

The question is, does one continue with the contract in place? Or does one take steps to break the contract? Can all contracts even be broken?

Whilst the twin flame issue runs deep into the fractality and complexity of the matrix (as in, everyone has a twin flame, no-one has a twin flame, everyone is one's twin flame and yet more perspectives) it is the actual matrix and the geometries (the contracts) we speak about at this point.

For if a marriage is a contract moving through many dimensions along the vertical line of the matrix, so may be the infiltrations and hijacking from those who have the software to enable them to hack into your matrix field.

The twin flame issue is close to everyone's heart, for all in physicality yearn for the answers to physical love and soul love. For the purposes of this transmission we return to the subject of soul contracts and how to find liberation as a master of your matrix.

3. The Linear Perspective Within the Non-Linear Reality

So let us look at the contracts made from the non-linear, non-physical perspective.

Within the 'non-linear' (as in 'outside of physical reality'), there is still a linear perception when your third dimensional brain tries to make sense of a multidimensional concept. Your brain, the interface for processing, must process in a linear sense. So let us look at the non-linear (still within the linear perspective).

So on that linear level, one could perceive the contracts are made from God, Source, or a higher self vantage point. Indeed this would be correct. A very aligned way to view this would be to visualise a higher council or collective of light beings making choices on your behalf regarding such things as experience, situations, emotional growth, physical changes, spiritual epiphanies and expansion, magical meetings, the codes for synchronicity and the meaningful subjective experience in place, node points, set triggers and all the mathematical equations making sense and standing in symmetry.

This is the state of the matrix at your birth into physical incarnation. Some of you may come in with unresolved traumas, blocks and energetic issues in place, set for resolution at a certain time (that in itself is the contract).

Even the imbalances fit into place mathematically when the incarnation begins. Hence the knowing that all infants at birth are pure, are innocent are 'little buddhas' in their own right.

Due to the unresolved issues that are set to mirror a matching frequency in the current lifetime through the blueprint of the matrix, the infant babe is seen as being 'born into sin'.

Both perspectives are correct yet use terminology that can be upgraded in your current timespace field.

Ancient lessons through text, script and talk have their places and their uses. Nothing is wasted in any reality, in any time. All hold use at some level.

So one sees the 'Council of Light' (for want of a better title) planning, creating and putting geometries into place. Each incarnation prepared for with such precision, such dedication and such absolute service.

In linear terms it would take a thousand lifetimes to make such an intricate preparation, yet all takes place within the 'blink of an eye'.

This is done for every soul leaving the 'collective of souls' and moving into an individualised physical incarnation. Regardless of realm, dimension or planet, the matrix holds strong.

Even within non-free will incarnations, there is a matrix of experience. Yet we digress, for that is a whole other subject!

So we view this 'Council of Light' hard at work, in contemplation, high energy, service and love, devising plans, coordinates and maps for entire lifetimes.

From the linear perspective this is what happened before you were born into the 'you' that you are now!

4. The God Self Contract and the Zero Point

What then, occurs from the non-linear perspective? That which we know as the 'Zero Point'?

From the Zero Point there can be no 'higher council of light beings', designing a lifetime prior to the birth of their physical third dimensional counterpart. That is a linear presentation.

From the Zero Point there is only now, only Source, only oneness, only unity. Does one need to leave the physical experience and the actual incarnation to experience this unity?

The answer to that is a resounding no! The central point of the blueprint itself, the matrix itself, is to experience the Zero Point and merge with the God self, Source perspective.

This is the ultimate 'past life contract' if you will. This is the contract you made with God, with Source. The contract was that you would incarnate in the physical dimension, experience the illusion of separation, pass experience and knowledge back to Source and within that, remember you are Source and return to unity.

One does not need to leave the physical body and move through the death experience in order to merge in a unified sense with Source and fulfil the God self contract.

One experiences this (in a non-linear sense throughout a linear journey) whilst still in incarnation. For that experience *is* the God self contract.

This is one contract one would not break and one that cannot be broken. The God self contract is in all realities, all thought and all dimensions.

Yet as we discuss the non-linear, one comes to the realisation that having a contract is, in itself, a linear presentation.

Therefore when one moves into the Zero Point, there is no God self contract. There are no contracts at all. For there is only what is. There is only 'you'.

When one moves into the Zero Point, one can then 'play within the fields of distortion' if you will, and move out of the central core of the fractal into the outer rings and change the matrix. This is the place where you break contracts and create new ones. This is the place where you remove smaller geometries from the larger wheel and add new sections of geometry to the overall dodecahedron presentation.

This can be done from the now, right now, wherever you are.

At this point it is impossible for another entity to 'hijack your software' if you will. The blueprint can be changed only by you.

A massive, impenetrable firewall moves into place within your matrix-computer-organic-technology field. This is liberation at the cellular level, for at this point there is a physical reaction. Your entire DNA structure is woven into the matrix computer technology that stands as 'all that is you' at the deepest levels, the *true* you.

The DNA is the physical structure yet there is much more to the matrix. It is an entire resonance field.

What takes you into mastery over that matrix? Or should we say within the matrix? Awareness. Expansion. Emotion. The awareness of bodymind. The expansion of your energy field. The emotion of love. There are many ways we can present this. Just the words themselves hold the frequencies to take you into the zero point. And thus into mastery within the matrix.

Feel the resonance when you speak these words.

Awareness.
Expansion.
Emotion.

Allow yourself to feel what these words truly mean and listen to your DNA sing with absolute recognition of 'all that is' as you say these words to yourself.

Awareness.
Expansion.
Emotion.

There are no Contracts

So to look once again at your first question...

What are past life contracts?

They are contracts or agreements made either in an incarnation or from the non-physical aspect. The contracts are made with self or other beings both human and non-human/ultra-dimensional/extraterrestrial/ angelic/elemental, etc.

Contracts are made with or without conscious awareness of making them. Contracts are made by a higher council of light, or from the full awareness of self within an incarnation, or from a non-physical linear perspective.

True awareness of these contracts comes to us when we fully understand that *there are no contracts.* This multidimensional thought process, coupled with true, deep and profound love for 'self and other' takes us into the Zero Point field.

From this point we attain 'mastery of the matrix' as we can choose to recreate new contracts, break old contracts or operate from a contract-free zone. It is from this point that we attain liberation of self as we cannot be infiltrated, hijacked or controlled. For there is only 'us' when full awareness of self takes place.

Magic

There is no other, only a unified field of all that is. This is the place where the magic happens. This is the place where the greatest creativity occurs, where the highest manifestations are birthed.

This is the place of no resistance, only pure allowing of flow.

It is in the Zero Point that we have no needs, no desires, no fears, no issues, no worries and no contracts. It is within the Zero Point that we truly find ourselves and it is here we discover that we are no longer the seeker, for nothing is sought after, nothing is found. There is simply what is.

5. Node Points

We come now to your question...

Why would we make a contract?

You ask the reason for these contracts in the first place?

Awaken your multidimensional eye for the answers are multilayered, multi-levelled and multidimensional.

Why indeed would we make a contract? And more to the point, why would another being want to make a contract for us?

For what reason would the software within our matrix field be hijacked in order to create a contract for us?

We shall respond to these questions.

Regarding the 'why' of making a contract, this is something that happens 'automatically' if you will.

It is the merging of 'energy with energy' in order to create the web, grid or matrix. The blueprint for incarnations is held within the matrix. The matrix is the 'personal Akashic Record'.

A complete 'holographic replica' of the universal, cosmic Akashic Record, the 'library of Source'. All time and all space converging as one. One could call this a seventh dimensional field yet, in truth, this permeates all dimensions.

The contracts and agreements made are the filaments, electrical wirings, connecting one aspect of the grid to the other. The contracts are created so that you may experience that which you need to experience for your highest good.

'Infinite possibility' is the material used to connect these filaments and 'finite probability' is the contract itself. Yet the contract can also exist within infinite possibility along with the 'there are no contracts' Zero Point paradigm. We speak here of the paradox of free will and destiny for *both* are contained within infinite possibility.

Like branches of a tree this intricate pattern of information, the matrix, grows around you and within you. It is you, it is your soul, your soul's blueprint. The mirror image of Source. Individualised consciousness. You are the manifested organic matter of the matrix grid.

The contracts are the filaments, the connections. They are the 'node points' within the blueprint. When walking the blueprint of incarnation there are many possibilities, many fields you may explore, many courses of action you may take as you make your life choices within each incarnation.

The node points are the convergence points, the contracts made. These are the points one experiences in all timelines. One could see these as 'points of graduation' if you will. For each time you reach a node point, all information accumulated within the incarnation at that point is 'stored'. We could liken this to a 'save point' within a computer game.

The guidance system around you, the archetypes from the grid, the 'mind of the matrix' (the archetypes being the individual personalities of that mind) will 'lead you' towards these node points.

Synchronicity is the matrix energies working to draw you towards the node point. The node point is the convergence. All experiences at that point within the incarnation are evaluated.

They are sorted, analysed and re-experienced. All on a non-physical level, experienced outside of linear time.

The moment of analysis, sorting and re-experiencing is instantaneous. This feels to you like a 'shift' in your life, a rebirth or an epiphany. Or it may not be recognised at all. Yet it is a significant point in your incarnation. As you awaken and become more and more aware, more activated, enlightened and ascended, more and more node points are experienced.

Until such time as your entire incarnation becomes a node point. The node point is the Zero Point, the contract with Source, the ultimate awareness and state of being.

The silence.
The stillness.
The knowing.
The oneness.

This is the point of **unity with Source.**

The node points may be 'small' if you will. Perhaps a meeting with a particular person? The reading of a particular book? The dreaming of a dream?

Or the node points may be 'large'. The visiting of a particular sacred space? The creating of a creation that reaches many others? The group gathering upon a sacred day?

In truth all node points are the 'same size' yet their perception by you is different.

Each node point is a contract. Each particular individualised energy field (person, animal, situation, entity) will have been party to the creation of that contract.

The contract is the node point. The Zero Point experienced within the incarnation. The contract is the 'merge point', the moment where self meets self, where the matrix of Source and the mind of the incarnated physical entity merge and become one.

The contracts are created, as ***this is the way creation works.*** It is a collaboration of one aspect of Source with another aspect of Source. Or perhaps we could put it thus... it is a collaboration of one aspect of self with another aspect of self.

Therefore we could say that the reasons the contracts are made, are in order for you to move into situations and energies within your incarnation that will assist you in the highest expansion at that point.

This is indeed true, yet the absolute reason the contracts are made is because **this is how creation works.** You cannot exist within the third dimension without creation, for you **are** creation.

You cannot exist within the third dimension without the node points, for they are the very fabric of reality. You cannot exist without these contracts. Yet remember the unified perspective within the Zero Point? When one sits upon a node point? At this point **there are no 'contracts'** and at that point 'you' cease to exist.

For 'you' become oneness. All that is. Source.

Your journey within reality is a journey of merging the third dimensional self with the higher dimensional self.

Therefore you cannot experience the third dimension and all the growth and expansion it has to offer without the node points.

Yet you cannot move into enlightenment unless you experience the Zero Point and move beyond the node points.

Or should we say, move **into** the node points? At this moment the node points cease to be linear. There are no longer an infinite number of node points but only one. The one you now exist within and experience.

Integration

It is said that you are not humans having a spiritual experience, you are spirit having a human experience. Yet in truth, both of these statements are correct.

You are human, treading the linear platform, walking the linear path and looking upwards and outwards as you embrace the archetypes of the higher mind.

You are spirit, spiralling through time experiencing all and everything. From this point there are no archetypes, only you, only self, only 'all that is you'.

You separate yourself into 'holographic cohesive sections'. You fragment, you scatter. In order to move back together into a state of integration. Becoming individually whole. Standing as a 'God self' in your own right. Within sovereignty. A God self amongst many God selves. A realised being. Yet as *unified* as one can be. Connected with the all. At one with all things. Experiencing *one mind.*

This brings us to the question, why would another entity want to hijack your matrix and create contracts on your behalf that are not for your highest good?

They do this in order to prevent sovereignty. To prevent full realisation of self and to prevent the development of the new God self that is you. Why do they wish to do this?

6. Hijacking the Matrix

The opposing polarity to self, *'service-to-others'* self... is self, *'service-to-self'* self.

Service-to-others moves towards *sovereignty for all.* The circular, spiralling geometry that moves and flows through the universe. Seeding itself again and again in an act of creation.

Service-to-self moves towards power for self, and self alone. It individualises at the top of a pyramidical structure, it is interested in seeding only self, as the *only God self*, with other entities in service to it.

Service-to-others geometry is a creational act that mirrors Source. It is an act of *alignment.* It is a unified geometry. A symmetrical geometry.

Service-to-self geometry is a destructional act of *distortion.* Its geometry is that of the 'power' and the 'powerless'. It is a fragmented geometry. An asymmetrical geometry. It provides the 'polarised contrast' for service-to-others.

The 'power' cannot retain its structure without 'the powerless', therefore *there must be the powerless* (from the service-to-self perspective).

The powerless aspect of the structure is absorbed by the power aspect of the structure. The entities created from this structure are therefore 'self absorbed', they must absorb self in order to exist.

Service-to-others hold 'other' as self. They give to that self as if that self were themself.

Service-to-self hold 'other' as a means to increasing their own power. They 'absorb' from other.

Only when 'other' holds an identical geometric print to 'self' will that 'other' not be absorbed. Neither is the 'other' served but is groomed or trained to take the place of self, as the new topmost point of the pyramid.

On a physical incarnate level we refer here to those who have retained the service-to-self pyramidical, geometric power structure within the bloodlines.

Therefore the 'son' and the 'daughter' aspects of this individualised self will not be absorbed but shall be preserved.

Only if the preservation leads to an *absolute mirror of the original self* will the preservation continue. If the preservation moves into a different course or gravitates towards a service-to-others frequency, then the preservation will be absorbed (or absorption will be *attempted* – it is not always successful).

We are looking here at a divided structure that thrives upon obedience and loyalty rather than freedom and respect. The geometries are similar, yet in complete opposition in their structure.

Both geometries are called into existence, by creation, within a third dimensional reality, planet or world in order for *contrast* to be provided. Contrast creates growth and expansion. When a third dimensional reality, planet or world nears *completion* the beings within that reality begin to polarise, create new dimensions or 'splits' within their worlds and begin to experience the reality they are polarised into.

Within your reality there are service-to-self incarnated beings, service-to-others incarnated beings and a whole spectrum of frequencies in-between. We would refer to the frequencies in-between as 'neutral', or 'unpolarised' ('neutral' and 'unpolarised' refer to different frequencies for 'neutral' is not the same as 'unpolarised'). There are also 'partly-polarised' beings.

The reason the matrix is hijacked and the contracts are created by the service-to-self structures, is in order to prevent sovereignty. The contracts are node points that *confuse* rather than *create* clarity.

They are 'false contracts', containing false presentation. The entity is led astray by presuming he or she is following a light of sorts, yet the light is 'false light', catching the soul into a net as a fish is caught in the ocean.

The soul returns again and again through the fourth dimensional wheel back into a physical incarnation upon Earth. This provides sustenance for the pyramidical structures of service-to-self, the powerless entity is then absorbed by the self absorbed, its energy fuels the service-to-self structure rather than its own. The matrix is hijacked, the false contracts are created and the entire incarnational journey of the powerless structure is controlled.

This is what has happened to humanity upon Earth for thousands and thousands of your Earth years.

For humanity itself, this creates the most contrast away from enlightenment and oneness, therefore this situation acts as a springboard back into enlightenment and oneness. It is most natural for you to feel angry, violated and controlled when you first discover the depth of control that humanity has been subject to.

However, and this is most important for you to know, process and understand, your emotion is the tool that has been used to hijack your matrix.

We repeat, for this is so significant. *Your emotion is the tool that has been used to hijack your matrix.*

The matrix, as we have said, is a giant computer that surrounds you. You input information and signals into this computer all the time and the computer generates scenarios and situations in direct response to the information and signals you feed into it!

The information and signals you give to this giant computer are delivered via your emotional field. It is your *emotion itself* that is the information. It is your emotion itself that is the signal.

Therefore, if one is not controlling the emotion, one is not in control of the signal that is being sent to the computer, the matrix.

Yet there is another important perspective to this. All emotion is part of your learning and growth. To try to 'control it' is to suppress it. Suppressed emotion is a most unhealthy and unaligned state for the incarnated human to exist within.

Therefore the emotion is to be felt. It is to be acknowledged and it is to be learned from.

Then the emotion is to be transmuted, integrated and placed. When this is done, one is in a state of flow. When one is in a state of flow, it is the state of flow that is input into the computer as information and as signal, *not the original emotion.*

It is the outcome of the processed emotion that is the signal.

Only when emotion is felt without acknowledgement and understanding does it become the signal for the computer.

When the emotion rages through the body, without recognition of what it is or why it is there, only then does it become a signal for the computer matrix.

When the emotion is ignored or repressed it becomes a signal for the computer along with the frequencies of ignoring and repressing the emotion. Those frequencies also become the signal for the computer matrix.

When the emotion is 'skipped over' or bypassed, it becomes a signal for the computer along with the frequencies of skipping over and bypassing.

What we mean by 'skipping over' or 'bypassing' is the conscious repressing of the emotion, glossing over the emotion with another emotion with the belief that the original emotion should not be felt.

This skipping over or bypassing allows for the replaced emotion to also act as a signal for the computer matrix, creating a 'mixed reality' for that individual. This is inherently a more desirable pattern for the human soul yet it is still a form of repression.

It is integration one is looking for.

Firewall in place

If one wishes to stand in sovereignty, with a firewall in place within their computer matrix so that the signal cannot be hijacked, *one must integrate the emotion.*

The metaphor of the firewall is also a temporary one whilst you learn the discipline and study of emotional integration.

There shall come a time whereby the firewall is no longer needed, for the computer software is simply unreadable for those who would look to hijack it. The firewall is no longer necessary at this point. For all metaphors are replaced with pure energy when one enters the Zero Point field.

7. Emotional Integration

How do you integrate your emotions, so as to send information and signals to your computer matrix that serve your experience as souls?

How do you create the patterns necessary to prevent hijacking of your matrix?

How do you create the firewall?

When you feel an emotion, rather than acting upon that emotion immediately, ignoring it or totally burying it, you allow yourself to sit with that emotion for a while.

When you come to the decision that the emotion you are feeling is an emotion you should not be feeling (so you cover it with another, more acceptable emotion) allow yourself to sit with the emotion for a while.

You allow yourself to go through the process of *emotional integration.*

The first step is to acknowledge the emotion one is feeling. For example, if this emotion is 'anger', one can say to oneself, "I feel angry." This is the acknowledgement of the emotion.

For those who work with archetypes, it is most helpful and in alignment to create an archetype for the emotion you are feeling. For those very sensitive, intuitive souls amongst you, one can allow the archetype of the emotion to come to you.

For example, the emotion of anger may present as a dark entity, a shadow person or a small dark coloured 'bear like' or 'spider like' being. It may simply be a colour or a frequency or a shape rather than an archetypal presentation. Whatever comes to you, accept this presentation.

To 'name' this presentation is most helpful. This can be an actual name, or one can simply call the archetype by the name of the emotion, as in 'anger' or 'angry'.

The next step after acknowledgement is analysis. One would take steps to discover the *reason one is feeling* the emotion.

One recognizes the emotion is there to tell you something, or to show you something.

In the case of archetypes, one would show gratitude towards the archetype for coming into your reality. In essence, you are thanking the emotion for being part of you. Thanking the 'persona' of the emotion for being there.

This is a major step into integration. Thanking the archetype or persona will in many cases create dissolution of the emotion altogether.

The analysis may take many forms. Therapeutic writing, dream work, meditation or contemplation, whichever form of analysis works for you or *feels right* to you.

Shadow Trauma

Within this analysis, one may decide that they *do not know why* they are feeling a certain emotion. If this is the case then you are working with a buried issue or 'shadow trauma'. The more 'unravelling' you do through analysis, the more the reasons for the emotion in the first place will make themselves clear to you.

Within the analysis may come many realizations, and other emotions may come up for you.

The gratitude, forgiveness and other resolutions to the original emotion are healthy aspects to the overall analysis. They are healing and are *not* the same thing as replacing or bypassing the emotion with another.

Yet it may be, in time, that you become adept at moving through the stages of emotional integration very quickly. In which case it may seem as though you are bypassing or replacing the original emotion. As long as you have been through the steps of recognition/naming, gratitude and analysis, then this is a healthy process that sends an aligned signal to your computer matrix.

The signals you send are those of integrity, spiritual commitment, discipline, alignment, growth and expansion as well as the emotions expressed, as you move through the unravelling process of emotional integration. These emotions are the signals sent into the computer matrix. The geometry of the matrix then re-sets itself accordingly, giving out matching resonance signals into your manifested reality.

The events that then occur for you are an absolute energetic match to the signals broadcast by your matrix. Many know this as the 'law of magnetic attraction'. Indeed, it is this law we refer to.

Yet presenting the field around you, the matrix, as the conductor of the frequencies and signals brings you into a 'higher' or 'more accurate' metaphor, for this is the *field of the DNA* which broadcasts the signal. The DNA being much more than chemicals and compounds that exist within the cells and the blood within your body.

The DNA is part of the mind, that which we call 'the bodymind'. The matrix we speak of is the 'externalised energetic field' that surrounds you as well as running through your entire physical body. This matrix is indeed 'you' in a higher dimension. Most specifically (depending on reality model used), the sixth dimension.

Your emotions and your thoughts are therefore key to the projection of that field and the signals it broadcasts.

Integration of emotion prevents the service-to-self entities from hijacking your matrix for *integration is not sustenance for them.* The sustenance they look for is a particular frequency.

The frequency they look for is *fear.*

8. Acknowledgement. Gratitude. Analysis. Integration.

When a human physically incarnated being feels fear based emotion (fear, lack of self worth, anger, guilt, jealousy, defensiveness, spite and so on), without any recognition or integration, the emotion is broadcast directly into the computer matrix as a signal.

The computer matrix then responds accordingly, creating a matching geometry that draws experience and energy into your reality that matches the geometry.

There are many teachers upon your planet that have taught this 'law of magnetic attraction' as a philosophy, indeed a correct one.

Yet this has been interpreted in many ways leading to feelings of guilt within many individuals whenever they feel a fear based emotion.

This occurs when individuals only partly understand what the law of magnetic attraction actually is.

They think to themselves, "I should not be feeling this emotion," or "I am failing spiritually because I feel anger." (or irritation, jealousy, fear and so on)

This has also led to many individuals finding fault and criticism with other individuals who feel fear based emotions, saying to others, "You are not progressing because you still feel fear," or "Rise above your anger, for all you need is love."

This in itself negates the positive emotion that the negative one is replaced with. This creates a lack of self worth and a 'lack of competence' feeling within the individual who experiences the fear based emotion.

It gives them a sense of failure.

For individuals moving through a path of enlightenment, expansion and ascension, this sense of failure is most detrimental to their journey. For the feeling of having failed at the one thing that is most important to them, their very spirituality, creates a geometry that within the matrix is broadcast as despair, shame, inferiority and hopelessness.

The geometric patterns set within the matrix are fear based emotional pattens that exactly fit the frequency the service-to-self entities are wanting to utilise as energetic sustenance, for they are in direct opposition to power and sovereignty.

They mirror exactly the frequency of powerlessness.

We say to you now that you have not failed. You do not fail when you feel anger, guilt, fear or jealousy. These emotions are as much teaching tools for you as the love based emotions are.

The archetypal presentations to fear based emotion such as gremlins, demons and vampiric beings are as much teachers for you as the angels, ascended masters and light beings are.

We repeat this for it is so significant...

The archetypal presentations to fear based emotion such as gremlins, demons and vampiric beings are as much teachers for you as the angels, ascended masters and light beings are.

It is how you act upon these emotions that affects your matrix and thus your reality.

It is how you respond to and interact with these entities that affects your matrix and thus your reality.

Acknowledgement.
Gratitude.
Analysis.
Integration.

The release that so many of you feel, when you discover that it is perfectly fine to feel a negative emotion, is profound.

Many of the informations you have been presented with as spiritual teachings on your planet have been misunderstandings and misinterpretations from the well meaning spiritual teachers and conduits of light themselves.

This has been an issue of interpretation. Yet, also there has been deliberate distortion of truth and disinformation presented to you from the service-to-self entities.

Another method of hijacking your computer matrix field.

9. Bliss Charged Love

So now you are aware of why contracts are put into place, what they are, what service-to-self frequencies are and why they aim to hijack your matrix, change the signal broadcast and create contracts that bind you into a cycle that provides sustenance for them.

We come to the subject now of moving into the Zero Point field and becoming masters of the matrix.

We have shown you how emotional integration is a powerful tool in creating the aligned frequencies within your matrix field. What frequencies exactly do they align with?

We speak here of the frequencies known as love and light. We refer to these frequencies as 'lovelight' and 'lightlove'.

Within your spiritual teaching field the phrase 'love and light' has become most popular. Yet it is misunderstood by many. There are those who reject the phrase of love and light for they see this phrase as having no substance, no meaning.

They see this phrase as a sign that the person using the phrase is ungrounded in reality, and this may be so in all truth.

Yet 'lovelight' and 'lightlove' are geometric codes. The phrase 'love and light' creates a geometric code that fires directly into the matrix field creating an instant clearing or upgrade.

Lovelight and lightlove are very high geometric frequencies linking into the golden frequency, that which is known as the 'golden mean' or 'golden equation', also known as 'the Fibonacci sequence'.

It is the mathematical equation of creation itself.

Lovelight and lightlove are frequency codes for the 'Golden Mean' inner resonance. The emotional mirror to this is ***bliss.***

Lovelight is the emotion of bliss combined with the infinite intelligence of the universe. Lightlove are the frequency codes of awareness and intelligence that combine with the emotion of bliss. Both of these equations lead to that which we call 'bliss charged love'.

Yet one needs both lovelight and lightlove in order to move into the Zero Point field. The frequency of lovelight and lightlove is fired into the matrix field through your blending, merging and balancing of these frequencies.

Lovelight and lightlove are very similar frequencies when experienced by physical incarnated humans. They are 'two sides of the same coin' if you will.

Both create a 'bliss charged love' activation, yet lovelight alone and lightlove alone are not enough to move one into the matrix field and become masters of the matrix. One must have both, blended, merged and balanced.

The emotional feelings of lovelight and lightlove are so similar, even the highly sensitive ones find it most challenging to hold these frequencies long enough to appreciate a difference between them. Yet here, we will present to you emotional triggers through visualisation of the imagination fields of hyperspace in order to assist you in feeling, integrating and firing the lovelight and lightlove geometric codes into your matrix fields.

Lovelight holds *love* as its foremost emotion. The visualisation of the 'pink rose' is a most appropriate visualisation for the love aspect of lovelight.

The love within lovelight gives power to the light. Therefore we are looking at the emotion of knowledge. The emotion of knowing, which equals bliss charged love. The golden mean frequency within.

Lightlove holds *knowing* as its foremost thought. The visualisation of the 'holy grail' (in whichever form comes to you) is a most appropriate visualisation for the light aspect of lightlove.

The light within lightlove gives knowing to the power of love, the love moves into a place of 'receiving' which is a feminine place. The love within lightlove is feminine.

The love within lovelight is masculine.

The visualisation of the **pink rose** and the **holy grail** are most aligned visualisations for the frequencies of lovelight and lightlove.

Imagine, if you will, the two objects placed upon a table in front of you. If you have envisaged the holy grail as a frequency then hold that frequency in front of you, by the pink rose upon the table.

In your visualisation you would pick up the pink rose first, in your left hand. Then take the holy grail in your right hand.

Stand strong, in balance, knowing you hold the frequency of lovelight within. Imagine the frequencies created by the pink rose and the holy grail are moving into the matrix grid around you. You can utilise the visual within the imagination fields of the computer. You can see yourself inputting information into the computer and you can allow yourself to see, in your mind's eye, a digital picture of the pink rose upon the computer screen.

You would then go through this exercise in reverse.

Visualising the holy grail and the pink rose upon the table. Taking first the holy grail with the left hand, followed by the pink rose in the right hand. Holding knowing of the frequencies of lightlove firing into your matrix field.

Inputting information into the computer and first seeing the holy grail upon the screen, followed by the pink rose.

The Language of Light

What you are doing here is communicating with the DNA matrix utilising a very ancient language. A cosmic language. Understood by all beings and all consciousness structures. The language is that of *frequency.*

Like 'radio wave bands' if you will, or perhaps musical notes. Each frequency is a letter of that 'cosmic alphabet' that makes up this language. We call this 'the language of light'.

There are symbols known to you that hold the matching resonance to the frequency, each symbol stands as an 'alphabetical numeral' within the language of light.

The pink rose holds the frequency of the love within lovelight. The holy grail, however you visualised it, holds the frequency of the light within lightlove.

The frequency is 'understood' by the DNA matrix. The subconscious mind recognises the symbol as it is passed from the left hemisphere of the brain to the right, and the frequency of the symbols processed.

This language, whilst cosmic and universal (indeed multiversal) is unique to you. For it is your emotional resonance created by the symbol that creates the frequency.

Therefore, one symbol for one individual may create a different resonance field than that of another individual.

The more aware, awake, activated and expanded you become, the clearer this language of light is for you. Even though the language is unique to you (the symbols appearing the same, creating the same matching resonance fields as one another), we can see that amongst those who receive our words now, the symbols of the pink rose and the holy grail are processed with matching frequencies to lovelight and lightlove.

Bliss charged love is the resonance created by the integration of lovelight and lightlove. The language of light is your key into this recognition, utilisation and integration.

Therefore 'bliss charged love' and the 'language of light' are both most significant aspects within your enlightenment and ascension journey into becoming a master of the matrix.

10. Ascension

When you integrate and balance lovelight and lightlove through the language of light, and you create the bliss charged love frequency within the matrix, you enter the Zero Point field.

Within the Zero Point field, the matrix can be changed. New contracts are created. Cleansing, defragmentation, order, categorisation, filing, streaming and shifting is undertaken.

However this is done shall be unique to you and there are many, many paths to this mastery.

What you are doing here, within the Zero Point is essentially *moving into a unified field of consciousness.*

Within this unified field you become 'all things', you *are* all things. You return 'home'.

You do not need to leave your physical body in order to access the Zero Point (although that has been the usual path to enlightenment upon your planet thus far).

There have been individuals who have reached the God realised state of mastery whilst in incarnation. Those individuals have moved into the process known as *'ascension'.*

Currently upon your planet Earth a *collective ascension process* is being experienced. There are a great many of you moving through this process now. This is the process of returning 'home' whilst still in physical incarnation. You move into this state of unity with all things, the 'unified field of consciousness' also known as the Zero Point field.

When you do this, you can change the codes within the matrix and thus the codes within the DNA.

The DNA codes, currently the double helix carbon based formation, move into the triple helix crystalline based formation. This means the codes within the DNA change the energetic structure of the physical vehicle from matter into antimatter.

Physical organic matter alchemises into pure light. This is the 'ultimate alchemy' as it is the golden mean frequency that runs through your entire organic system when you reach this Zero Point full actualised state.

The 'alchemist' and the 'master of the matrix' are one and the same.

The triple helix crystalline formation is one of multidimensionality. It is where all aspects of self are available to the physical incarnated human vehicle. They are no longer viewed within the linear field (as incarnation after incarnation along a past, present, future equation), all aspects of self become one. This is the re-integration after the dis-integration.

The physically incarnated individual must dis-integrate (as in separate all aspects of self in a sense of breaking down) aspect by aspect within a circular, spiralling, fractal geometric pattern.

When this is done and the individual becomes Zero Point activated, the re-integration takes place. The 'new' individual is then birthed into the DNA crystalline structure, allowing that which you know as 'higher self' to stream into the fields of the individual in human incarnation.

When this happens, the process is known as 'activation of the light body' or 'rainbow body of light'. This can also be referred to as a 'walk-in', 'activating the Merkabah vehicle' or 'kundalini raising'. It is also known as **'ascension'.**

This is the journey you are on. You would not have found your way to our words unless you were on this journey, for the information itself is a resonance field, finding its way through the waveband of synchronicity to its like vibrational match. ***You*** or rather ***'your thoughts'.***

11. Free Will and Destiny

Your thoughts are the vibrational match. We have spoken of the emotion and how the emotion creates a resonance field that sends codes and information into the large computer around you, known as the matrix.

The resonance field of the emotion and the vibrational match of the thoughts, when in alignment, when carrying the same frequency, are the geometric pattens needed for manifestation. For whenever a thought and an emotion are in synchronised frequency with one another, a creation is birthed from that.

The majority of humans amongst you, on your planet at this time, do not hold a synchronised resonance between their thoughts and their emotions. Occasionally this may occur for them but this resonance is not understood on a conscious level.

Once this resonance is understood on a conscious level then it can be utilised with full knowing and full awareness.

We see that the individuals amongst you who are going through this process, known as the 'ascension', are moving into the emotional, thought synchronistic resonance more and more often.

It is not a linear process. You move in an out of this Zero Point field as you expand and grow. Oftentimes you may feel as though you are taking a step backwards, forgetting your spiritual teachings or losing your grace and spirituality. This is a most 'normal' feeling for those on an ascension path. Yet this is the way the awakening, awareness and expansion works.

This brings us back to the node point we have spoken of. The node points are convergence points where timelines within your blueprint converge together.

Each node point is a point within a spiralling, geometric pattern within your blueprint, rather than a linear line.

Each node point is an 'entry point', if you will, into the Zero Point field. Each node point is a portal to the Zero Point.

The node points are convergence points in all timelines when you incarnate as the consciousness that is *you* in physical form. These node points, whilst being major synchronicity or 'meaningful coincidences' are also known to you as 'destiny', 'fate' or 'serendipity'.

When you reach a node point in your life, you have the feeling that 'all is as it should be' or 'all is meant to be'. It will feel right to you. It will feel *in alignment.*

If you are on a conscious spiritual path to awakening, enlightenment and ascension, you will feel that sense of 'absolute decision' about this point in your life. When we say 'absolute decision' we mean the moment where you feel that your life has already been decided.

It is at this point where you may start to ask questions within your reality regarding your own free will. For if all things are already decided for you, already predetermined, how can there be free will?

We say to you that 'free will' and 'destiny' walk hand in hand, but what exactly does this mean?

When one enters the node point in one's reality, that point indeed has already been decided (predetermined prior to incarnation), yet this is the point you enter the Zero Point field. The Zero Point field is a non-linear field of consciousness. The moment that your individualised matrix grid is fired into the 'Source field' if you will. There is no past, present or future here.

Therefore, although the 'higher self' or 'higher council of light' (the aspect of you that is multidimensional and exists with the 'collective frequency of Source') made the decision for you regarding this node point, prior to your incarnation, when you sit upon the node point in your reality *you* make the decision in that very moment. *You* decide your reality, your life, your destiny from the 'here and now' aspect within your physical life.

When 'on a node point' you *are* the higher self, higher council of light and the collective frequency of Source.

The service-to-self constructs and beings within that vibration know how to 'hijack' the matrix of the sleeping, unaware, third dimensional thinking humans, creating contracts for them, superimposing 'true node points' with a 'false screen' (if you will) within their matrix field.

A false screen designed to cut them off from higher expansion and growth and keep them existing within a third dimensional thought process. They hijacked this signal and thus the individual's matrix, through emotion. They hijacked this signal through *fear based emotion.*

When fear based emotion is prominent (without analysis and integration), it keys into the matrix creating a mirrored match of more fear based emotion, within a reality that appears to cause and create scenarios and situations leading to fear based emotion.

When fear based emotion is prominent, and predominant, the true node point cannot be accessed. This is caused by non-recognition and dismissal of the true node point.

If the paradigm of the individual is a fear based, 'ego self' based reality, then node points do not exist for that person for they simply cannot be seen.

Yet all service-to-others vibrations within the matrix field of the individual will be constantly creating the mirrored match to the service-to-others vibration.

No matter how much the service-to-self energies hack into the matrix signal and create false screens within the node points, they cannot wipe out the service-to-others frequencies.

They will always be there. Hence the reason why many third dimensional thinking humans feel as though they have a 'devil' on one shoulder and an 'angel' on the other!

This is also the journey of the 'higher self' versus the 'ego self'.

All are one and the same. All explain the service-to-others and the service-to-self signals trying to polarise within the matrix field of every individual.

Service-to-self polarised beings can only hack into the matrix of an individual already holding service-to-self frequencies within their matrix. They can only hack into the matrix of an 'unpolarised individual'.

Once the service-to-others frequency has polarised within an individual, and lovelight and lightlove has begun to balance within the individual's matrix fields, then the service-to-self energies and beings can no longer hack into the matrix of that individual.

12. Polarisation

How does an individual polarise into a service-to-others vibration?

The polarisation takes place when an individual holds predominantly service-to-others frequencies within their matrix fields. They do this through thought and emotion. If the thought process of the individual is predominantly one of unity (viewing all others as themselves), and if they exist within a predominant energy of service, surrender and allowing (they exist within a state of flow), then the matrix will be healthy and contain an abundance of light codes.

Everything within the individual's reality works together in a cohesive motion to polarise the individual into the service-to-others vibration for everything influences and contributes towards thought and emotion.

The behaviours, situations, people, verbal expressions, environmental influences, nourishment, movement, dreams, entertainments, music and other sound vibrations and visual images, all go towards the polarisation of the individual.

How does one prevent moving into a fear based emotion if the service-to-self energies and beings are hacking into the matrix fields?

They do this by creating scenarios within the third dimensional reality that are designed to create a fear based response. These scenarios are created throughout most social systems within your reality. So how does one prevent moving into the fear based emotion?

One prevents this by moving into the awareness and the knowing that the 'inner reality' has more influence over the energetic systems within your bodymind than the 'external social systems' within your third dimensional set up.

We repeat. *The inner reality has more influence over the energetic systems within your bodymind than the external social systems within your third dimensional set up.*

One prevents this by keeping healthy 'imagination fields of hyperspace spaces' and drawing joy filled/bliss filled images and emotions into dreamtime.

As much as the service-to-self energies and beings have hacked into the social systems to influence the matrix fields of humanity, the service-to-others energies and beings have provided that which we refer to as 'safe zones'. These are 'systems of light' holding service-to-others frequencies.

These systems of light are all around you, giving balance to service-to-self influence.

The systems of light holding service-to-others frequencies are to be found within the same places as the service-to-self frequencies.

Within the social systems, the service-to-others frequencies are not so 'obvious' (if you will) to the third dimensional thinker, yet they are there in situations, people, places, buildings, nature, art, music, literature, digital and cyber-reality, nourishment and other entertainments.

They are there in energetic exchange between like-minded, aware individuals.

For each service-to-self influence, there is and shall continue to be, a service-to-others influence to counteract and balance.

One becomes accustomed to 'tuning their antennae' into the systems of light and the service-to-others frequencies, rather than the service-to-self frequencies.

This creates the healthy, flowing 'matrices of light'.

We see the 'aware ones' (such as you who receive our words) are creating these matrices of light and are holding these matrices of light.

What does it mean to have a 'healthy' matrix? Does this suggest a fear based frequency within the matrix is unhealthy?

13. The Healthy Matrix

We use the term 'healthy matrix' to describe a matrix that is 'Source aligned', as in one that flows in symmetrical balance with lovelight and lightlove frequency.

The healthy matrix is the one held by the organic human, he or she who lives in harmony with your planetary body, the Earth.

The 'unhealthy matrix' is one filled with an asymmetrical pattern with blocks, holes, dark patches and has a lack of flow.

Yet each physically incarnated human holds the codes within the matrix to be able to shift from an unhealthy matrix into a healthy one.

This brings us to mention the large telepathic community of lightworkers, lightwarriors, wanderers, starseeds, indigo, crystal and rainbow individuals, gridworkers, mapmakers and teachers of ascension, each moving into an awareness leading them into 'mastery in their field' and to become masters of the matrix.

These individuals are the healers amongst you. They are those who offer themselves in service to the light and thus to the collective that is humanity. These individuals live their mission as healers to others. Their calling is to assist and help others, and this calling has been an activated code within their matrix since their birth into this incarnation.

If 'you who receive these words' feel stuck, lost and alone yet so desperately want to unfold and expand into the energies we speak of here, to become masters of the matrix, yet you are confused and do not know where to start, we say to you... seek out one of these healers for you have but to ask.

Simply think of the healer, the teacher, the guide upon Earth that you need, that you resonate with at this time and you will be drawn into that healer's reality as the healer will be drawn into your reality, for the contract has already been made.

Meeting with this healer will be a node point for you, allowing you to access the Zero Point field and become a master of your matrix.

The healer may be literally a hands on healer practicing a healing template or form such as reiki, or other similar hands on healing templates.

He or she may use oils, massage and fragrances to assist with the healing frequencies coming through the hands. The healer may use other methods to balance the physical body such as herbs, fruits, seeds and other sustenance and nutrition.

The healer may be a healer of the mind rather than the body, utilising talking therapy, communication, words and language of light translations.

This 'healer' that you call into your reality by becoming an energetic match to their message, template or therapy, may not be a person. The message may present through the healer's creation such as music, artwork or written material.

The healer for you may be a book, digital presentation or digital visual artistic work.

This healer may present as a physically incarnated animal, or you may access non-physical healers, guides, masters, light beings and collectives.

Yet when the healer and you are contracted together, you enter the node point when you connect; whatever form the healer may take.

14. Recap

What are preincarnate contracts?

These are geometric 'patterns' within your matrix that align with energetics within the third dimensional reality, that give you experiences and connections when you are physically incarnated into the physical body.

Why do we make them?

For many reasons, specifically expansion of soul by experiencing that which we need to experience on a soul level. Ultimately we make them because this is the way of creation.

How do we make them?

They are made by conscious verbal contract with another, within an incarnation or by an 'energy match' outside of physical reality, or both.

Who do we make these contracts with?

Another individual, or group of individuals, or with self, or both simultaneously. Past incarnation makes contracts with future incarnations (and vice versa). The ultimate contract being the contract with Source intelligence, prime creator, higher self collective.

Are we conscious of making them?

When an individual moves into an awakening or ascension experience, they become conscious of these contracts. Often the making of the contracts is not held within the memory system, therefore one could say from that perspective they are made without awareness.

Can they be made against our will or without our knowledge?

The answer to this is yes. We have covered this extensively, for this particular issue is the main subject matter of this entire transmission.

Can we break them?

Indeed, yes. This is done by entering Zero Point consciousness where there are no contracts, only self. This is the central point of the matrix and it is from this point that you are able to 'turn that wheel around you' and 'remake the matrix map' if you will.

Are they negative or positive?

The response to this is both. They are most positive, in the case of a twin flame connection, and indeed the connection with Source, moving you into your destiny, your mission upon Earth. If they no longer serve you and are 'outdated', or if they trap or bind you into a third dimensional linear reality that creates constriction rather than expansion, they are negative contracts.

How can we tell if we have any?

Just by incarnating into a physical form, within a third dimensional linear reality, there will be contracts formed.

However, there are now children incarnating who are 'karma free' if you will. We call these individuals the 'children of the third wave'. They hold only positive contracts within the seventh dimensional framework/twin flame energy.

Many of these 'children' are now teens and in their early twenties. Once an individual is able to access Zero Point states and stand within the central point of the matrix 'wheel', they too become 'karma free' and become masters of the matrix.

How do you break these contracts?

By becoming a 'master of the matrix' through Zero Point consciousness. This is achieved by following a spiritual path in life, moving into alignment with one's 'North Star' (the inner guidance system), and operating within the frequencies of awknowledgement, gratitude, analysis and integration.

How do you create new contracts?

From a place of conscious awareness and mastery over one's matrix. An incantation is provided for this very purpose within this transmission.

How can you tell the difference between a negative and a positive contract, and how do you know which contracts serve you and which no longer serve?

This is part of the journey into enlightenment and ascension. As you move into an expansive energy field within your reality, this shall become evident. The contractual frequencies and geometries shall be made known to you on a conscious level.

Following the 'North Star' (the inner guidance system) is the key.

Learning how to feel resonance and balance within. Learning how to tell that which does not resonate and does not feel balanced within. When one becomes a master of the matrix, one feels the geometric balance within self and can feel the contracts.

Each contract may also come to you as an archetype, or perhaps a book or computer disk within the Akashic library of all that is, overseen by the cosmic librarian. You can ask for this information to show itself to you within your visualisations and your meditations.

A meditation to access the Akashic records regarding your preincarnate contracts within the matrix is provided within this transmission.

<u>What is the 'firewall', the software needed to prevent the matrix from being hijacked?</u>

The 'firewall' is the pattern of sovereignty, and any stream that leads to sovereignty such as integrity, love/light, light/love, bliss charged love, joy, abundant confidence within one's creativity, forgiveness, compassion and ultimately gratitude.

The geometric frequency of gratitude creates the pathways within the matrix field for sovereignty. When an individual operates from these patterns & geometries (emotions), they create the firewall.

Their matrix cannot be hacked, infiltrated or changed by any entity; save self. The individual becomes an integral unit within sovereignty.

15. Chakra/Matrix Connection

We come now to a suggested method of creating a stream or conduit into the matrix field to 'fire up' (or more accurately *'phire up'*) the matrix grid. Perhaps we could also say 'lighten', 'cleanse' or 'clear' the matrix.

There are several ways one can do this. Visualisation combined with emotion, grounded by ritual or talisman with incantation is a very effective way to do this.

One would visualise the stream or conduit connecting oneself to the matrix grid field that surrounds the body.

In truth the matrix grid field is within you and *IS* you. You are *always* connected, but creating a visual 'feed system' which speaks to the intelligence of the cosmic DNA within, by utilising the language of light communication, will assist you to *'phire up'* the matrix grid.

So, for the purposes of this exercise, one would visualise the connecting stream or conduit. This can be visualised as golden thread connecting each of your chakras to different parts of the matrix grid field surrounding you.

Or you could visualise the silver cord connecting at your solar plexus chakra, and feeding into the matrix grid field.

Another visualisation would be a white light above your head at the crown chakra, connecting with the matrix.

Or a stream of pink light connecting from your heart chakra into the matrix grid.

Whether you use just one of these visualisations, all of them together, or your own metaphoric visualisation, *the conscious connection with the matrix will be made.*

Crown connections will be associated with multidimensional

communication, heart connections with unconditional love, bliss/joy emotion, and solar plexus connections with power, psychic ability and intuition.

An 'all chakra' connection will be associated with the rainbow spectrum of self and the rainbow body of light activation.

Your intuition, your inner knowing, will lead you to the most aligned visualisation for you (which may change each time you do this exercise).

You would then consciously allow yourself to feel joy/love/bliss within your emotional field (or as near as you can find within the emotional scale of self).

As an actor finds emotion within which to portray a character upon the stage or screen, so too do you find that emotion. Worry not if it does not seem 'real' (as in you are superimposing joy over despair/stress, etc), this is NOT bypassing such as we spoke of before. This is for a specific exercise which *will* have the desired effect when this is conscious. As in the case of an actor portraying real emotion, yet not standing within a field of resonance to create a law of attraction reaction.

The universal magnetic intelligence is aware of the difference between 'real' emotion, bypassing/superimposing emotion, and emotion as part of the language of light.

You are using the third option here. You are utilising the emotion in conjunction with an aligned visualisation in order to communicate with the cosmic DNA via the language of light.

If you cannot raise the emotional field into love/joy/bliss, and you remain within a stress/despair/hopelessness state, then it may assist you to remember a time when you did feel contented, happy, joyful, in love, in a state of celebratory rejoicing or bliss. Projecting oneself into that memory whilst utilising the visualisation of the chakra matrix connection will have the desired effect.

If tuning, chanting a mantra or listening to uplifting music helps you achieve the joy/bliss/love state, then go ahead and do this.

The ritual/talisman is the physical object to be used as a grounding tool, directing the energies into the third dimension. An object meaningful to you is suggested. Yet be aware that objects hold frequency, and the frequency within the object will be the frequency with which the energies ground themselves into your physical reality.

For example, the use of a childhood toy that has comforted you throughout the years. The energy of sorrow, or whichever emotions you were feeling each time you turned to that childhood toy, will be attached to the toy.

Objects of 'high power' are most recommended. These are objects that are known within the collective field of humanity as being 'spiritual' or 'magikal' objects. Such items as candles, crystals, natural stones, sea shells, ornamental fairies, unicorns or dragons, crystal wands, skulls, feathers, tarot and oracle cards, organite pyramids, jewellery and so on.

Be aware that each object holds frequency, so again, come back to your intuition.

Using a clear quartz crystal, a crystal wand or skull would be most in alignment with this exercise and most recommended! However, we would recommend advanced magikal workers only use these objects due to their focused amplification properties. These are suited to beginners *ONLY* when that beginner has an absolute link with higher self collective within full auditory or clairvoyant connection, so may be guided through working with objects of high power.

The same is said when utilising tarot cards (although oracle cards are suitable for beginners).

The tarot holds a specific frequency, and only advanced tarot users are recommended to utilise the cards as the grounding object within this exercise. Each card holding specific energy depending on which energetics you wish to directly feed into the matrix field.

The most neutral objects would be a white candle, a white feather or a crystal (rose quartz, blue lace agate or amethyst). These are suitable 'high power' objects, not influenced by the collective consciousness of humanity.

White objects especially hold 'high purity' and neutrality within service-to-others light as 'high power' objects.

Following your intuition regarding chakra/matrix connection, emotional love/bliss pattern and grounding talisman, one would begin the incantation on the following page (or similar in one's own words or as directed from one's higher self collective/ascended master/guidance system).

THE INCANTATION (The Golden Ark)

I cleanse and spin my fields.

I allow my matrix to settle within symmetry and purity throughout the dimensional scale.

I project my most loving thoughts into my matrix fields.

I project my highest compassion into my matrix fields.

I project my utmost joy into my matrix fields.

I project my Zero Point, bliss-charged-love templates into my matrix fields.

I stand within knowing of the Golden Ark running through my fields.

I welcome the golden pattern.

I stand within the all, beside the all, and as the all.

I hold my matrix as the conductor, conducer and creator, beaming light within a healthy superimposed geometric wheel.

So that it may carry me forward to all place and space for the highest good of my tribe, my soul and the one true soul.

I am... (your name)

Speak your actual name, or magikal working name, when you make your 'I am' statement at the end of the incantation.

So therefore you have the method.

The physical body responds to the conscious awareness you create by vibrating at the frequency of the golden mean equation/Fibonacci sequence. The DNA spins and moves into a 'higher formation'.

This is the 'original template for man', known also as the 'goddess template' or 'the 12 strand DNA formation' (or the 144 strand quantum DNA formation, depending on viewpoint), or indeed the 'crystalline matrix.'

"I welcome the golden pattern."

This reinforces your willingness to embrace the golden frequency at the cellular level. You move into the 'archetype of the alchemist' at this point. Known also as 'goddess alchemy,' or 'alchemy of the gods'.

"I stand within the all, beside the all, and as the all."

You hold full awareness of your God self/Source self, and you communicate at the deepest levels with your DNA. The left hemispheres and right hemispheres of the brain are balanced and you move into the 'divine marriage' of the feminine and masculine aspects within.

"I hold my matrix as the conductor, conducer and creator, beaming light within a healthy superimposed geometric wheel."

Once this part of the incantation is spoken you stand as an 'instrument of the divine', receiving a much higher percentage of 'Source awareness' into your being.

You are no longer a third dimensional human being at this point but are an 'evolved human' operating from multidimensional consciousness. You take your part within full individualisation and integration whilst simultaneously embracing unity.

"So that it may carry me forward to all place and space for the highest good of my tribe, my soul and the one true soul."

You 'broadcast this signal' of an individualised and integrated self, whilst fully embracing unity on a conscious level, into all awareness of space/time and time/space in your reality and beyond your reality.

You give the activation template for this into the 'consciousness grid of light' for all to receive. You create a map for others to discover, decipher and follow.

As the individuals that access this map and follow this map grow in numbers, you create a 'critical mass field' and it is at this point that a new dimension is created upon your planet.

When this happens upon third dimensional Earth, it also occurs on all the other planets and throughout all the dimensions. A planetary and dimensional upgrade takes place. This creates a 'memory', 'knowing' or an 'understanding of experience' for Source itself.

This 'dimensional upgrade' is how Source begins to know itself. We say 'begins' because the knowledge Source seeks is always 'at the beginning', for the knowledge is infinite.

In truth there is no beginning, no middle and no end to the knowledge and the knowing that Source seeks. Source seeks to answer the unanswerable question which is "Am I conscious?" or "Do I exist?"

"I am... (your name)"

As you state your name, following the words 'I am', you seal and ground your manifestation.

You have created a 'hermetic seal' here. Once created, the seal itself takes on its own life, creating its own geometric field and its own matrix. The realisations or birthings that come from the hermetic seal and your high level manifestations (as the wizard, the magician, the warrior, the wise man or wise woman, the artist, scribe, professor and the alchemist) strengthen the individual frequencies of the archetypes within, simultaneously merging all selves, all aspects, all archetypes together to create a new archetype.

An archetype that you consciously hold and embody as you walk the rest of your blueprint within an Earthly reality. An archetype to imprint upon your very soul (the matrix) and carry it through to all incarnations, experiences and points of perspective.

As you read our words and process their meanings, and the DNA within responds to the activations given here, you shall embody this new archetype.

What is the new archetype?

It is 'Master of the Matrix'.

17. Questions for the
White Winged Collective Consciousness of Nine

In reference to the material within this transmission,
can the Nine respond to some questions?

1) What is 'timeline jumping' and how is it connected to the matrix and mastery over it?

Timeline jumping would mean exactly that. 'Jumping' from one timeline to another. However, it does not exactly work that way. A more accurate model to explain this would be when timelines converge together within a node point.

We speak here not of your personal preincarnate blueprint, but of the timelines. That which we would call probability fields, merging together as part of the cyclical nature of time.

These are therefore 'planetary' timelines rather than individual 'soul map' timelines (although in truth they are one and the same).

When these convergence or node points occur, then individual probability fields blend together (or wrap around each other or superimpose upon one another) causing a 'bleed-through' from one timeline to another.

During these intersections of timelines, one can project one's consciousness into the conscious experience of one's alternate self, therefore 'jumping' timelines.

This is a natural part of evolution and creation and it happens all the time, although you are collectively much more aware of this since your ascension culmination point of the winter solstice, December 21st 2012.

This is connected to the matrix by the fact that 'the planetary matrix' is a complete holographic map of probability fields based on the collective consciousness of humanity (as in 'humanity's collective thoughts').

The 'individualised matrix' is a complete holographic map of probability fields based on your own individuated consciousness (that of the individualised aspect of you).

As we have said, in truth, the planetary matrix and the individualised matrix are one and the same. Yet they are perceived very differently as one is the result of 'you' (your thoughts and your frequency) as an individualised point of perspective, and the other is the result of 'you' (as in 'all that is you', being your collective thoughts and collective frequency as a planetary race) as a collective point of perspective... but still you!

Attaining mastery over your matrix is therefore attaining mastery over your timelines, not only as an individual soul but as a collective planetary group.

This is significant due to the fact that there are several probability fields concerning your planet and humanity's future and, as a 'master of your matrix', you can consciously choose which future to experience and actively and consciously create your planetary reality.

When several individuals hold the same vision for the planet and for humanity as a whole, then this adds 'weight', 'strength' or 'power', if you will, to that vision and lines you up as an energetic match with the timeline that holds that experience for you.

Currently, you collectively hold the vision of Earth and humanity taking their places within a 'galactic society' where that which has been hidden from humanity for a great many years is finally revealed. This is the reality most likely to occur at this time for all who hold that vision.

2) Are the 'node points' the same as Zero Point?

Yes, in effect. The reason for this is the node points, during the moment of convergence or intersection, create a 'nullifying equation' moving 'finite probability' into 'infinite possibility'. This creates a moment of opportunity for humanity (most especially for 'aware' humanity). We call this moment of opportunity a 'stargate'. For as you connect within Zero

Time (the nullifying moment of intersecting and converging timelines), your controlled and consciously directed thoughts (focused intention) merges with the fabric of creation. This makes the probability of the focused intention becoming manifested actuality, very high, especially if a critical mass point within humanity has been reached at that time. However, individuals have just as much ability to create individual reality if they hold 'accurately focused intention' combined with a pure heart, as in 'pure intention'.

3) Do you create your reality by living in alignment with node points?

Absolutely! When one becomes aware of their place in reality, who they are, why they are here, and they live a life of 'spiritual discipline', one learns to follow one's inner guidance system and one's inner alignment to light/love and love/light. The node point will therefore be 'reached' at the exact same moment as the wish/asking/desire.

Therefore, these 'stargates' are created within the individual's reality at the exact time they are needed. Windows of opportunity will present themselves through divine synchronicity. An individual living this way lives a life of 'magic'. They have become 'the magician', 'ascension architect', or indeed the 'master of the matrix'.

4) Do new scenarios in life create new pathways within the matrix?

When an individual is living a conscious aware life (as in 'walking an ascension path'), then new scenarios and new pathways within the matrix are created simultaneously. This is the exact same phenomenon as living in alignment with node points, making decisions and choices in life at the exact same time as you create the probabilities for the outcomes of these decisions and choices (prior to multidimensional awareness).

One would perceive this as 'new scenarios creating new pathways within the matrix', or indeed 'new pathways within the matrix (created by your thoughts, emotions and actions) creating the new scenarios in your life'!

5) Is 'the matrix' the same thing as the human brain?

The human brain is an 'interface' for the matrix. The human brain interprets the matrix and is a mirror or 'holographic replica' of the matrix.

The matrix, however, is far more than the human brain (when perceived within third dimensional linear thinking) as it encompasses all of one's reality. As you become more and more activated, aware and 'crystalline' your human brain will be able to 'fully map the matrix' more and more.

From that perspective, one could say it is the same thing when looking at the geometry and frequency it presents. The most accurate way to explain the synergy between the brain and the matrix is to use the metaphor of your 'computer'. The human brain is the 'hardware' and the matrix is the 'software', yet you need both to create a computer. They work together to create an information device, or antennae, to receive information.

6) Is 'the matrix' the same thing as the DNA?

The answer to this is yes. The DNA, that part known to scientists as 'junk DNA', or known to esoteric and spiritual philosophers as 'etheric DNA', is the matrix.

7) If you cannot create a new scenario within your life, then can you superimpose new scenarios upon the matrix through thought structure or belief system?

Yes. This is a very good technique for healing and for bringing oneself into balance, as well as manifestation. Ultimately this is a tool that is useful for bypassing 'actual experience' as a way to 'balance karma', by experiencing the contrast and polarity needed for your growth and expansion as a soul within an 'imagined scenario' rather than an 'actual scenario'.

Your human brain, as the interface for the matrix, interprets signals from the matrix. It makes no difference if these are actual experiences, 'dreamtime' or 'imagined' experiences.

In order to provide aligned, balanced superimposed scenarios that are an energetic match to the actual experience, one would be an adept at this work. One would be a 'master of the matrix' and would change the 'original blueprint' from a physical experience in matter to an 'astral' or 'hyperspace' experience within antimatter.

As long as the emotional imprints and frequency are a vibrational match to the experience, then the 'karmic lesson' is learned.

Utilising the very fabric of the matrix, the building blocks of reality known as the 'platonic solids', one can create a geometric 'hermetic seal' to create an 'energy enclosure' or 'Faraday cage' as a containment field for this work.

This is also known to you as working within your Merkabah vehicle. We break down the Merkabah vehicle into language of light, geometric frequency for you, in order to present you with the geometric, mathematical patterns with which to create this.

If you look at the letters within the words MER-KA-BA, you are instantly given the codes within which to create the containment field for this work. Trust that which comes, your DNA (matrix) knows and understands this for you speak this language, the language of light. This is not something that can be done incorrectly, you cannot 'get this wrong' for the creation of the MER-KA-BA is unique to you.

The interlocking star tetrahedrons or pyramid structures are the most usual geometries that come into your visual field when working with the Merkabah. A perfect union of the sacred masculine as the male creative energy, and the divine feminine as the female creative energy.

When the Merkabah is 'activated', you may see a spin around this geometry or even feel a spinning motion around you or within you. For some, the Merkabah may change shape as the sides stretch outwards and the top and bottom parts of the Merkabah move closer together, resembling a spaceship.

Those who work with archetypes may see a winged being, or indeed may feel as if they are carried along by a winged chariot, or indeed by Pegasus the winged horse.

Language of light symbology may present that you are 'riding upon a magic carpet'. However the Merkabah presents to you, this signifies spiritual 'movement' or interdimensional travel or motion.

This is the activation of the light body and the movement you feel is the 'spin' of the matrix, or indeed the 'spin' of the DNA. This indeed is the 'spin' of creation.

Language of light coded poetic presentations such as 'Dreamweaver, Weave Your Dream' or 'Weave Your Web', or storylines depicting the spinning wheel or the spinning of straw or cotton into gold, are all triggers to Merkabah and matrix activation, and the movement into the new geometric rainbow light body, the crystalline self.

There are Merkabah masters upon your planet who teach this work in depth but in truth, there is no wrong or right way to 'create' or 'call' the Merkabah when one holds alignment to trust, knowing, surrender and a pure heart.

8) Are mandalas the same thing as the matrix?

Mandalas are visual representations of the matrix, yes. Presented as a visual trigger, through artistic means, they are a most useful and aligned tool to work with. Pick one that resonates with you within its patterning, or work with several. Indeed create your own but yes, the mandala is the matrix.

However, mandalas are presented as the matrix as a whole, yet also as a singular geometry as in 'one section' of the matrix. The matrix is a large web of interlocking matrices therefore 'many mandalas' may represent the matrix in a more accurate way than one singular mandala.

However, the mandala is a two dimensional picture of a fractal. Therefore if you visualise the mandala in a three dimensional form, you have an accurate representation of the matrix and of reality itself.

The mandala is a powerful and magical tool to work with, for you utilise the language of light in a very profound sense when you work with the mandala. To look at pictures of the mandala, wear jewellery or other talisman depicting the mandala, or have tattooed mandala artwork upon your person, is a deeply magical and transformative act.

Individuals are often mesmerised by mandalas, drawn to them without knowing why. For when you work with the mandala, through the language of light, you stand in conscious awareness of the matrix. This is a major trigger into the crystalline change and the activation of the light body. For each mandala contains 'codes', if you will, that work through the language of light to communicate to your matrix and DNA grid system about your inception, incarnation and entire soul's mission.

The most powerful language of light symbology that can be utilised through the mandala, and work with the mandala, are those based on sacred geometric symbology, the Kabbalah and, most significantly, 'Metatron's Cube'.

9) When you hold the mandala flat and then imagine you pull it outwards into a ball, then a wheel, then into a tube or vortex, is this the same thing as the torus? Thus the DNA?

Again we respond yes. We have already spoken of visualising the mandala in a three dimensional sense, and if you were to continue to view the mandala from several angles and visualise the mandala as being pulled into a tube or vortex, then yes, this is the torus and the DNA.

This is exactly what we mean when we speak of the matrix. As you can see, the matrix can be 'viewed' in many different ways from different perspectives. Each shape the matrix takes on within your fields of visualisation creates a trigger for DNA activation, for the cellular physicality incarnated within matter, mirrors the etheric probabilities and creational webs within antimatter.

The torus or matrix is a wave form of energy. It is fluid and ever moving, not static, in response to your thoughts, emotions and overall frequency. As a master of the matrix, you will be able to utilise 'pure focused intention' to create clear flowing fields of balanced, rainbow light tori around you, which in turn give out the signal of liberty and sovereignty that you wish to hold as a crystalline multidimensional being.

10) How is 'Metatron's Cube' significant in relation to the matrix?

Metatron's Cube along with several depictions of the Kabbalistic tree of life, are the most accurate representations of the matrix.

Metatron's Cube, the containment field, Faraday cage or hermetic seal that contains the building blocks of life, the platonic solids, is a two dimensional image of reality. Metatron's Cube shows you the entire dimensional presentation, along with space/time and time/space, matter/antimatter, and non-duality/unity.

Working with the geometric presentation of Metatron's Cube is a major activation tool for matrix awareness, light body creation and the crystalline formation.

To 'decode' Metatron's Cube, one can look mathematically or artistically. One can create music, stories or poetry inspired by the geometry of Metatron's Cube. Or one can work directly with the 'ascended master archetype', the archangel Metatron.

If one stands as a conduit or channel and communicates well with non-physical beings, then Metatron is a most aligned consciousness structure for matrix activation work.

If one wishes to work directly with Metatronic energy, one would visualise the geometry as three triads of light, with the top most triad or first triad as the 'home of Metatron', if you will.

One can work directly with the geometry itself by meditating upon the image of Metatron's Cube. The image of Metatron's Cube is a key, a trigger to the doorways of consciousness. Each and every one of you will 'read' or 'map' Metatron's Cube in a unique way, and again there are no incorrect or correct methods of deciphering the codes of the cube. All the answers to the questions you may ask are contained within the image of Metatron's Cube.

Metatron's Cube is the absolute representation of you as 'the alchemist' and it is the code for ascension itself.

The Kabbalistic tree of life, and its various depictions, is simply another version of Metatron's Cube viewed from a different angle or perspective. A representation once again, of that which we call 'the matrix'.

The tree of life displays the dimensions as spheres, so one is looking down upon reality as if it were a spiral.

Metatron's Cube displays reality much like the matrix, as a series of interlocking matrices within a giant pulsating web. Yet you are, in truth, looking at the same thing.

One could say that Metatron's Cube gives an 'overview of reality' with step by step instructions to creation itself, and the tree of life gives an overview of reality with the dimensions (or indeed the various stages) of life. Or the activations that occur within the human energy system and chakras as a predominant expression. But both show the 'matrix of Source'.

We, the White Winged Collective Consciousness of Nine, present to our conduit, Magenta Pixie, as nine white winged beings or angels. However, our more accurate forms would be geometric.

We are three triads superimposed upon one another, or stacked on top of one another. Metatron's Cube is a formation we move into alignment with, as are various depictions of the Kabbalistic tree of life.

We are the matrix system of our conduit, Magenta Pixie. She is able to communicate with her matrix system, us, just as you are able to do the same. We may present as geometric formations, light, colour rays, pure energy or nine white winged angels. Either way, we are the matrix system of our conduit yet in truth, we are the matrix system of the entire oversoul of our conduit.

We are known by many names.

We are known as the 'White Brotherhood', the memory structure known as 'RA', the group soul known as 'Ashtar' or 'Ishtar' and the service-to-others, positive polarised aspect of the Luciferian angelic sixth dimensional structure.

All of these presentations are different versions of us and who we are, and we are part of all Pleiadian and Arcturian starseeded sixth dimensional ascending structures of reality.

We hold a Venusian and Lyran inception point, with a close creative link to the Andromeda system and the constellation of Sirius. In various different patternings and formations, each of you that hold activated memory and the energy of the wanderers or starseeds hold very similar energies. All of these truths of your origins, forms and signatures can be discovered by working with the matrix, through mandala, Merkabah, tree of life, Metatron's Cube and matrix work.

11) What is the 12 strand DNA star/crystalline matrix, or twelfth dimensional gateway?

This is the 'seed point' for the highest expression of the matrix that can be achieved whilst you are still incarnate within a third dimensional reality. Although indeed, you will be existing within a geological 'fourth density' when you activate the 12 strand DNA formation or crystalline matrix.

We say 'seed point' because the energetic frequency of the crystalline activation expands as you move forward with an Ascension process. What is happening here, is the crystalline matrix changes form as you move through these stages of activation. Saying that the crystalline matrix 'expands' or 'opens up' is the best description we can give you based on the terminology within our conduit's fields.

An aligned phrase to use here would be 'fractal transformation within frequency raise'. For the musically minded amongst you, we could say that you would 'begin to hear the unheard note'. For the artistically minded amongst you, we could say that you would 'begin to see the unseen colour'. Yet the best way to explain what actually happens to you, as a physically incarnated human, is to look at the memory you hold. We specifically refer to that which we call 'higher memory'.

The twelfth dimensional gateway is the convergence point, or node point, of timelines holding the template for the positively polarised fourth density experience.

The 12 strand DNA formation is the regrouping of all the 'memories' of all your incarnations, from the moment of your inception point as an individualised soul.

This is the first template of 'higher memory', for it is at this point that you have access to all incarnations and memories from inception point within a soul's linear expression.

Once the 12 strand DNA formation is complete, one will move into the quantum sun crystalline matrix, which is the blending or merging with the central sun for your planet. This is the regrouping of all the 'memories' of all your incarnations from the moment of your inception point as a collective or group soul.

This is the second template of 'higher memory' so, for example, if 'you' as a linear soul held an inception point within the Pleiades then 'you' as a collective or group soul may hold an inception point within Arcturus, Lyra or Venus.

For your inception points are several, not one, from the multidimensional/quantum viewpoint.

Once you have accessed this second template, you will hold a 144 strand DNA sun crystalline matrix, which is the quantum version of the linear crystalline matrix.

The third template of 'higher memory' is the Source point, prime creator memory. This is the regrouping of all the 'memories' of all your incarnations, up to the dimensional node point of convergence and intersection with the eighth dimension.

We would refer to this as the 'diamond matrix memory template', for at this point you are able to access all memories of Source; including the cyclical or spiralling inception and node points of Source creation, and the creation of your universe and galaxy. This is the perspective of a 'galactic creator' if you will.

There are many different ways to explain these stages of ascension, and this is not a linear process. Each step of the journey holds such wonders and such accumulation of knowledge, combined with the states of joyful reunion with your true star family, and the knowing of being within the bliss charged activated state. The 'golden' state if you will.

The twelfth dimensional gateway is also known as the 'higher blue ray', 'blue sphere stargate' or 'platinum ray'.

These three stages of crystalline and diamond matrix activations are geometric keys/codes/triggers given to explain the nine triads of the matrix.

The first three triads would be the 12 strand DNA star crystalline matrix formation, with the archetype of archangel Metatron as guiding light for that formation.

The second three triads would be the 144 strand DNA sun crystalline matrix formation, with the infinite intelligence of the central sun as guiding light for that formation.

The third three triads would be the fully realised diamond light body matrix formation, holding flower of life activated matrices within the blue sphere stargate/platinum ray. Also known as the 'rainbow matrix' or 'rainbow body of light'.

This is that which you know as 'Christ consciousness'; the blue sphere/platinum ray also known as the 'Christed sphere' or 'Christos sphere'.

All of these are metaphors for these activated, transformed energy states of ascension, utilising the language of light to communicate these energetics and frequencies to you in response to your questions.

12) Am I able to achieve this raise in vibration, and change in DNA formation into the crystalline matrix, and become a 'Master of the Matrix'?

Indeed this is the case, yes. You, humanity on Earth, are set for this evolutionary step. Or should we say 'leap'.

Codes for the new formation are all around you, and within you. We provide a meditation within this transmission as well as codes, keys and triggers within the transmission itself to aid you in this process.

Our transmission, "Masters of the Matrix", is but one trigger and there are many. You yourself are a potential trigger for others. For this activation is 'catching', shall we say, through a process we would call 'telepathic energetic resonance', or this may be known to you as 'sympathetic resonance'.

18. The Thirteenth Question

<u>It all comes back to you.</u>

What question has not been asked here?

Regarding the "Masters of the Matrix" material, is there anything left unsaid that needs to be said? If so, could the Nine comment?

Only this...

Those that infiltrate the matrix are <u>you.</u>

This has not been done *to* you, but *by* you. When you understand this, you free yourself and become master of the matrix.

When we say to you that there are those who would hijack your matrix for nefarious reasons, gain sustenance from your fear and prevent your sovereignty, we say to you that you live in a reality of polarity and of contrast.

You learn that which you need to learn by experiencing its polar opposite. You learn what it is that you want and need as a creative being by virtue of knowing what you do not want and need. This takes place on an individual level and a global, planetary level.

For you to experience growth and expansion at an exponential rate, you need to experience free will. There are universes that are non-free will universes, as such was yours in earlier times. In order to experience free will, you need to make decisions and choices. You cannot do this unless you know what you want and need.

A non-free will universe can be a love/light universe with only positive polarities. Whilst this is a beautiful place to exist, it does not allow for rapid exponential growth and expansion leading to transformation.

By virtue of experiencing 'that which you do not need or want', you discover what you do need and want. You can therefore make a decision or choice. Contrast and polarity must be provided along with free will to make those decisions or choices.

When you were the 'galactic ones', known also as 'game players' or 'designers' (we call these beings 'keepers of time' or 'reality architects'), you decided you would provide contrast for the beings of Earth. You decided that the beings of Earth would be given free will and would make their own decisions and choices, in order to facilitate the greatest growth and expansion.

Once you decided this for the beings of Earth, you yourselves incarnated into these beings in order to 'play your own game' (if you will).

Some of you chose to experience 'the game' as an individual experiencing free will, and therefore contrast. Others of you chose to provide contrast.

The individuals (physical humans, extraterrestrials and non-physical entities) that hijack your matrix for nefarious purposes are the 'you' that decided to incarnate and provide the contrast. These beings are not 'other', they are 'you'.

You incarnated into beings that wished to experience free will and contrast AND into beings that were to be given the task of providing contrast.

In order to leave the game, or should we say 'win the game', one needs to realise who they are and realise they are incarnated within both polarities. For that is the way of a free will universe within the third dimension.

Once you realise that you are both polarities, then you win the game.

How do you do this? By integrating *both* polarities within self. When enough of the gameplayers (you) have moved into this place of integration, then critical mass will be reached. When this occurs, polarity begins to dissolve. Or should we say *'resolve'.*

The key to this integration is *the acceptance of both polarities.*

The acceptance of both polarities is the understanding that you are not caught up in a victim/saviour mentality, but a mentality of love, understanding, forgiveness and empowerment.

There are those of you 'playing the game' who are not aware that they are playing a game of experiencing contrast and free will. There are those of you 'playing the game' who are not aware that they are providing the contrast within a free will universe.

These individuals are caught up in the game. They do not realise it is a game. They believe this to be reality, and all that reality has to offer. They are unable to achieve integration because they are caught up in the polarity/victim/saviour mentality.

Those that have realised they are 'playing a game' are able to have respect and love for those 'on the other side' (if you will).

They play their parts for they know it is their mission to do so, keeping hold of the greater vision within. They do not turn the other cheek to being controlled and hijacked. They stand strong. Yet when they stand strong, they do not do this from a place of hatred or a place of 'crushing their enemy'. They realise their 'enemy' is, in fact, their brother.

Indeed they realise their 'enemy' is self. Therefore they stand strong from a place of honour and integrity with forgiveness, love and gratitude in their hearts. Not gratitude for nefarious acts done to them, *but gratitude for the game and the chance to experience the free will and polarity that has led to their growth and expansion.*

So whilst it is important to be aware of your own sovereignty within reality, and keep the sovereignty codes balanced and activated within the matrix, it is also important to remember that 'no one has done this to you'.

You are not a victim. *You decided this for yourself.*

This is a difficult concept for many to embrace, and forgiveness is the main template for becoming aware of this truth. All aware individuals on 'both sides of the fence', shall we say, hold respect for the other and indeed support the other's mission even though their own mission is very different.

Awareness within both factions is rare but as it grows, polarity will lessen. For you, as a collective, have decided you no longer need polarity of this magnitude.

You have graduated beyond the need for polarity at this level. You are ready to experience a new plan and create a new game.

We bring you this transmission, ***"Masters of the Matrix"***, through our conduit, Magenta Pixie, so that we may assist you to do just that: experience a new plan and create a new game.

Indeed we wish you well, for you shall succeed in winning the game and creating the new game. Or should we say... you have won the game and you have created a new game.

For you are a ***Master of the Matrix.***

We are the White Winged Collective Consciousness of Nine.

"The Library of Records"

A meditation to accompany the "Masters of the Matrix" material

This meditation is for you to do by yourself. Please read through the meditation first, then find yourself a relaxing place to sit or lie down. Close your eyes, and then go through the meditation as you remember. Do not worry if the meditation is different when you move into your own visualisation. Whichever visualisations or images that come to you; these are right for you, at this time.

For complete beginners in meditation, we suggest you visualise a violet pyramid surrounding you before you begin.

Those accomplished in meditation may use their own Merkabah field, colour ray, or other familiar visualisation to take them into sacred space.

If you are a meditation facilitator and wish to use this meditation in a group setting, or if you are with a friend and wish to read the meditation aloud, then please use the script in the following section.

* * *

Within your meditation, imagine that you are standing before a large wooden door. The door has geometric symbols and hieroglyphs upon it.

Whilst you realise that these symbols and hieroglyphs are not your current language, you are aware that the symbols and hieroglyphs *are* a language.

They seem familiar to you.

You know, on some level, that you understand their meaning.

You are aware that the language presented by these symbols and hieroglyphs are inviting you to open the door.

You take a step forward and place your hand upon the large brass door handle.

You find yourself in a vast library.

The library contains many bookshelves, filled with books of all sizes and colours.

There are computers, laptops, tablets and other advanced technological devices.

As you stand upon the threshold of this large library, someone walks towards you.

A young woman, with brown hair walks up to you.

"I am Akashia, one of the librarians. How may I help you?" she asks.

You reply to Akashia, you tell her the reason you have arrived at the library.

"Please come this way," she says.

You follow Akashia along the vast corridor of the library.

She stops and points to another door.

The door is red. You notice a geometric shape upon the door.

The shape keeps changing.

The shape is blue for a moment, then green, then yellow, then orange.

The shape changes before your very eyes.

One moment the shape resembles a triangle, then a star, then a square, then a circle, then a diamond.

Akashia gestures for you to enter the room with the red door and the constantly changing geometric shape.

Once inside the room, you notice that there is just one book.

The carpet is red, the walls are a pale green.

There is one wooden table in the room and upon it is a large book. You walk towards the table.

The cover of the book is red. Upon the book is a very small geometric shape.

The geometric shape is gold, embossed into the red cover of the book.

Written on the book, in gold writing, are the words "The Records of..." - followed by your own name. You realise this is a book of your records.

You open the book.

The first page is entitled "Your Incarnations - Linear - Past Perception" and there you see writing, this strange hieroglyph writing, yet you understand what this means.

You realise that you are looking at writing that explains your incarnations in a linear sense; within the perception of being in the past.

Whilst you are in this meditation, think about what these words might say and visualise this. Take note of the information you receive visually and emotionally. You may hear softly spoken words in your mind, so pay particular attention to this.

You take some time to contemplate and decipher the hieroglyph language before you.

After a while, you turn to the next page.

This page is entitled "Your Incarnations - Linear - Future Perception".

You realise that you are looking at writing that explains your incarnations in a linear sense, within the perception of being in the future.

Have a think about what these hieroglyphs might mean. Take note of any information you receive here. Pay attention to visual images, sounds, spoken words or whispers, and emotional feelings.

You take some time to contemplate and decipher the hieroglyph language before you.

After a while, you turn to the next page. This page is entitled "Your Incarnations. Non-Linear - Multidimensional Perception".

You realise that you are looking at writing that explains your incarnations in a non-linear sense, within a multidimensional perspective.

Pay attention to the visual images you see once again. Take note of emotions, feelings and any memories that may come up for you.

You take note of all that you feel and all that you perceive, and you take time to assimilate and process this.

After a while, you close the book.

You turn around and walk out of the room, back into the main library.

A man is waiting for you in the library.

You do not need to remember the master librarian's speech word for word. Whatever comes up for you in your meditation is fine. The words here are simply a guideline or suggestion for when you move into your own meditation.

"Greetings. I am the master librarian, keeper of the records."

"Each time that you open your book of records, you may see something different. A snapshot of your blueprint. For what you see within the book of records are triggers, and the unravelling and processing of those triggers shall continue long after you have left the library."

"We await your return here, for you may visit the library any time you so choose. You may read any book you desire."

The master librarian bows to you. He smiles and continues with his duties within the library.

You return to the main door of the library.

You are fully aware of how much there is to explore within this vast library.

Thousands and thousands of books are available.

Computers, each with their own information.

And your own personal book of records; with ever-changing imagery and geometry, leading to an infinite abundance of knowledge.

Indeed, you shall return to this place. This you know.

You place your hand upon the brass door handle. You open the library door and close it behind you.

As you stand on the other side of the door, you begin to feel awareness return to your physical form.

At this point, allow the awareness to return slowly into each part of your body. You can bring your awareness consciously into each part of your body in turn, by wriggling your toes and fingers, moving your head, or stretching different parts of your body.

When you feel your awareness is fully back into the physical body, you can open your eyes and complete the meditation.

You can place your hands within the namaste prayer position, if you wish to do this; and give thanks to your higher guidance system (the intelligent cosmic consciousness that is 'the matrix') for assisting you with this visual journey within.

If you want to, you can take notes about any thoughts that came to you within the meditation that you feel are significant. Remember to have a pen and notebook next to you before you start, if you feel you will want to make notes.

"The Library of Records"

A meditation to accompany the "Masters of the Matrix" material

This meditation is written in a scripted format, for facilitators who wish to lead this meditation in a group setting.

* * *

Close your eyes.

(PAUSE)

Imagine, if you will, that you are standing before a large wooden door.

The door has geometric symbols and hieroglyphs upon it.

(PAUSE)

Whilst you realise that these symbols and hieroglyphs are not your current language (the language that you speak), you are aware that the symbols and hieroglyphs *are* a language.

(PAUSE)

They are familiar to you.

(PAUSE)

You know, on some level, that you understand their meaning.

(PAUSE)

You are aware that the language presented by these symbols and hieroglyphs are inviting you to open the door.

(PAUSE)

You take a step forward and place your hand upon the large brass door handle.

(PAUSE)

You find yourself in a vast library.

(PAUSE)

The library contains many bookshelves, filled with books of all sizes and colours.

(PAUSE)

There are computers, laptops, tablets and other advanced technological devices.

(PAUSE)

As you stand upon the threshold of this large library, someone walks towards you.

(PAUSE)

A young woman, with brown hair walks up to you.

(PAUSE)

"I am Akashia, one of the librarians. How may I help you?" she asks.

You reply to Akashia, you tell her the reason you have arrived at the library. "Please come this way," she says.

You follow Akashia along the vast corridor of the library.

(PAUSE)

She stops and points to another door.

(PAUSE)

The door is red. You notice a geometric shape upon the door.

(PAUSE)

The shape keeps changing.

(PAUSE)

The shape is blue for a moment, then green, then yellow, then orange.

(PAUSE)

The shape changes before your very eyes.

(PAUSE)

One moment the shape resembles a triangle, then a star, then a square, then a circle, then a diamond.

(PAUSE)

Akashia gestures for you to enter the room with the red door and the constantly changing geometric shape.

(PAUSE)

Once inside the room, you notice that there is just one book.

(PAUSE)

The carpet is red, the walls are a pale green.

(PAUSE)

There is one wooden table in the room and upon it is a large book. You walk towards the table.

(PAUSE)

The cover of the book is red. Upon the book is a very small geometric shape.

(PAUSE)

The geometric shape is gold, embossed into the red cover of the book.

(PAUSE)

Written on the book, in gold writing, are the words "The Records of..." - followed by your own name. You realise this is a book of your records.

(PAUSE)

You open the book.

(PAUSE)

The first page is entitled "Your Incarnations - Linear - Past Perception" and there you see writing, this strange hieroglyph writing, yet you understand what this means.

(PAUSE)

You realise that you are looking at writing that explains your incarnations in a linear sense; within the perception of being in the past.

(PAUSE)

What do these words say? What information are you receiving? What images do you see in your mind? What words do you hear, or feel placed within your mind?

(PAUSE)

You take some time to contemplate and decipher the hieroglyph language before you.

(LONG PAUSE)

After a while, you turn to the next page.

(PAUSE)

This page is entitled "Your Incarnations - Linear - Future Perception".

(PAUSE)

You realise that you are looking at writing that explains your incarnations in a linear sense, within the perception of being in the future.

(PAUSE)

What are these hieroglyphs saying? What do they mean? What information are you receiving? What images do you see in your mind? What words do you hear, or feel placed within your mind?

(PAUSE)

You take some time to contemplate and decipher the hieroglyph language before you.

(LONGER PAUSE)

After a while, you turn to the next page. This page is entitled "Your Incarnations. Non-Linear - Multidimensional Perception".

(PAUSE)

You realise that you are looking at writing that explains your incarnations in a non-linear sense, within a multidimensional perspective.

(PAUSE)

What do you see? What do you feel? What images come to mind? What emotions are you feeling? What words do you hear, or feel are placed within your mind?

You take note of all that you feel and all that you perceive, and you take time to assimilate and process this.

(LONGER PAUSE)

After a while, you close the book.

(PAUSE)

You turn around and walk out of the room, back into the main library.

(PAUSE)

A man is waiting for you in the library.

(PAUSE)

"Greetings. I am the master librarian, keeper of the records."

(PAUSE)

"Each time that you open your book of records, you may see something different. A snapshot of your blueprint. For what you see within the book of records are triggers, and the unravelling and processing of those triggers shall continue long after you have left the library."

"We await your return here, for you may visit the library any time you so choose. You may read any book you desire."

(PAUSE)

The master librarian bows to you. He smiles and continues with his duties within the library.

(PAUSE)

You return to the main door of the library.

(PAUSE)

You are fully aware of how much there is to explore within this vast library.

(PAUSE)

Thousands and thousands of books are available.

(PAUSE)

Computers, each with their own information.

(PAUSE)

And your own personal book of records; with ever-changing imagery and geometry, leading to an infinite abundance of knowledge.

(PAUSE)

Indeed, you shall return to this place. This you know.

(PAUSE)

You place your hand upon the brass door handle. You open the library door and close it behind you.

As you stand on the other side of the door, you begin to feel awareness return to your physical form.

(PAUSE)

Your awareness returns to your head, shoulders and neck.

(PAUSE)

Your awareness returns to your arms, hands and fingers.

(PAUSE)

You wiggle your fingers.

(PAUSE)

Your awareness returns to your torso and back.

(PAUSE)

Your awareness returns to your legs, feet and toes.

(PAUSE)

You wiggle your toes.

(PAUSE)

And when you are ready, only when you are ready, you open your eyes.

Enjoy this book?

Check out **magentapixie.com**

* Vast video archive of Magenta Pixie's messages
* Downloadable guided meditations
* Interviews, free stuff and more!

Videos by Magenta Pixie, available to view for free at magentapixie.com

1: Channelled Message from white winged consciousness of nine

2: The Mapmakers of the Ascension

3: Questions about Ascension Earth 2012 for the Galactic Source

4: Duality and Zero Point concepts in Ascension part 1

5: Duality and Zero Point concepts in Ascension part 2

6: Sacred Geometry in Ascension "The Triangle"

7: Reincarnation and Past Lives part 1

8: Reincarnation and Past Lives part 2

9: Our Starseeded Genetics and the Cosmic Grid - part one

10: Our Starseeded Genetics and the Cosmic Grid - part two

11: The Crystal Skulls

12: Messengers of Light. A call to Lightworkers and Starseeds.

13: Dark Matter, Dark Energy and DNA

14: Messengers of Light. The Lightworker's Mission.

15: Messengers of Light. Outer Space and Inner Space.

16: Messengers of Light speak of Meditation

259: Tea Time Chats: Episode 2 (Part 2 of 2)
Magenta, Jessica, Dee, Jean and Azra

260: Beat of the Drum (Stargate Key)

261: Twin Flame - Sacred Sexuality -
Interview with a soulmate fairy "Aphrodite's Apprentice"

262: Drums and Angels! "Tea Time Chats" Episode 3 (Part 1 of 3) -
Magenta, Jessica, Kelly and Heike

263: Drums and Angels! "Tea Time Chats" Episode 3 (Part 2 of 3) -
Magenta, Jessica, Kelly and Heike

264: Drums and Angels! "Tea Time Chats" Episode 3 (Part 3 of 3) -
Magenta, Jessica, Kelly and Heike

265: "Awakening to Genius" - Magenta Pixie interviews Zingdad

266: Dragon Energy (bringing in the light codes)

267: Tea Time Chats: Episode 4 "Talking Truth"
with Magenta, Jessica, Sheela and Ildiko (Part 1 of 4)

268: Tea Time Chats: Episode 4 "Talking Truth"
with Magenta, Jessica, Sheela and Ildiko (Part 2 of 4)

269: Tea Time Chats: Episode 4 "Talking Truth"
with Magenta, Jessica, Sheela and Ildiko (Part 3 of 4)

270: Tea Time Chats: Episode 4 "Talking Truth"
with Magenta, Jessica, Sheela and Ildiko (Part 4 of 4)

271: 2012 - The end of the world? Or a new beginning

287: 21st December 2012 - Stargate to the Golden Age
(Rainbow Light Codes Activation)

288: 21st December 2012 - Elemental Stargate

289: 21st December 2012 - Zero Point

290: The New 5D Light Body

291: 2013 - The Year of the Merkabah

292: Raw Living Food Lifestyle - Stargate into the Fifth Dimension

293: Musings with Magenta Pixie (full 150 minute presentation)

294: Inner Firewalk of Hyperspace - The Orange Ray -
The Ray of Fire

295: Your Birthday/Solar Return and the Cosmic Gateway
(Spring Equinox 2013)

296: Language of Light Stargate
(Love and Joy - triggers to creativity and communication)

297: Keycodes from Kuthumi - The Yellow Ray

298: Tarot & Oracle Cards, Totem Power Animals & Shape Shifters

299: Colour Rays, Language of Light Codes and
working with the higher metaphor

300: Crystal Skull Matrix, The Royal House of Avalon and
The God Complex

Also by Magenta Pixie...

"Elemental Dream" MP3 Guided Meditation Collection

Draw the elemental realm close through these channelled guided meditations from Magenta Pixie.

The elemental realm, a harmonic between the third and fourth dimensions, is an ideal place from which to create and manifest.

The archetypes you will meet within these meditations are aspects of the universal mind, presenting keys, codes and triggers for your spiritual awakening.

Utilizing the sacred language of the DNA, the "language of light", each archetype carries coded light language in the form of colour and symbol.

This communicates with your DNA, the aspect of you that holds the wider perspective.

The visual journeys through the fields of the imagination are keys to your own dreamtime.

Open to your own inner joy and love as you embrace the Elemental Dream.

INSTANT DOWNLOAD at magentapixie.com

Also by Magenta Pixie...

"Sacred Quest" MP3 Guided Meditation Collection

Journey through a rich tapestry of inner visions as Magenta Pixie guides you through enriching fables, mysterious landscapes and sacred soul teachings.

You are invited to embark upon an adventure, indeed a Sacred Quest.

Become a character in a story as you follow these guided meditations into the deepest recesses of your inner visionary potential.

The higher dimensional collective, The White Winged Collective Consciousness of Nine, bring forward these transmissions through their conduit, Magenta Pixie.

Each guided meditation is a trigger into your own DNA activation, expansion and healing.

Each meditation is, in itself, a spiritual journey.

Together, all seven meditations create the Sacred Quest.

INSTANT DOWNLOAD at magentapixie.com

Also by Magenta Pixie...

"Euphoric Voyage" MP3 Guided Meditation Collection

Magenta Pixie presents her "Euphoric Voyage" guided meditation collection.

Journey through inspiring landscapes of imagination and wonder.

INSTANT DOWNLOAD at magentapixie.com

Also by Magenta Pixie...

"Gateways Within" MP3 Guided Meditation Collection

A unique collection of guided meditations to
uplift, inspire, activate, cleanse and heal.

Suitable for beginners or advanced users, working on multiple levels.

Each person will receive what they need at that time, can be used over and over
again as you awaken and progress along your path to enlightenment.

The opening, closing and protective mechanisms are interwoven into the
meditations themselves. They can be used as guided meditations or listened to
during deep relaxation, hypnosis or sleep for subliminal activation, healing, stress
release and chakra balancing.

These meditations are especially created for individuals undergoing a conscious
ascension or evolution process and are for anyone who wishes to work on
themselves on all levels.

INSTANT DOWNLOAD at magentapixie.com

Also by Magenta Pixie... available to download at **magentapixie.com**

"Unicorn Ride to Kuthumi's Castle"

DNA Activation - Language of Light

Embracing the Yellow Ray / Cosmic Solar Plexus Chakra for
Higher Intelligence, Focus, Laughter and Play.
An excellent meditation for strengthening psychic ability
and fine tuning one's intuition.

"Key to the Language of Light"

A guided hypno-meditation to take you into a deeper level of hyperspace
awareness, so you may receive the Key to the Language of Light.

The merge and connection between the physical body and the Light Body is
triggered and DNA activation takes place as you connect with the fractal nature
and sacred geometry of the Universe and higher dimensions.

Also by Magenta Pixie... available to download at **magentapixie.com**

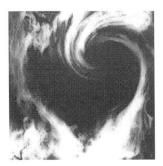

"Inner Firewalk"

Magenta Pixie presents "Inner Firewalk" - a unique 26 minute hypno-meditation for activating the Inner Rainbow, DNA restructuring into the Crystalline Change through the Cosmic Sacral Chakra (The Orange Ray - The Ray of Fire).

Upgrading, cleansing and balancing the chakras.

Moving into the multidimensional energy body (Merkabah Geometry).

Re-mapping the brain pathways into the "beyond the theta state" - triggering communication between the conscious and subconsious mind.

Re-birthing the Light Body through the Inner Firewalk of Hyperspace.

www.magentapixie.com

Made in the USA
San Bernardino, CA
27 September 2017